Space Encounters- II revised

An Underground *Principia*

About Me
and I

Margaret A. Harrell

Praise for the *Space Encounters* Series

Space Encounters III, rev. ed.—Inserting Consciousness into Collisions: A True Fantasy Adventure by the Earth through the Quantum-Entangled World

"Finally, a manual of the Universe but also connected to the deep psychology of the human being. In easy to grasp terms Margaret reveals insight into the processes that connect past, future and now; the quantum world with daily existence and seemingly superficial events with deep spirituality. The magic of this book is that it positions our place in the universe and our dream of life with much more clarity. A manual indeed."
—Jef Crab, Taiji master and Taoist

"This is a soul journey in and through and beyond space and time. All of Margaret A. Harrell's books are connected, linked. They are her never ending life story. Her new book is plugged in, an electric shock, a wake up call for those bold and daring enough to take the wildly delightful adventure to the whirling ever changing source of all and everything."
—Ron Whitehead, US Lifetime Beat Poet Laureate

"A wizard at turning the sign language of the specifics into messages of the beyond . . . A fantastic journey into the source of creativity. Another re-story-ing of how our lives are entangled in the grandiose web of the universe. This time taken from a myriad of perspectives: quantum leaps and how they shake up the Newtonian mechanistic worldview, Jungian archetypal wisdom seen from a quite unique angle, the huge impact on a life's course starting with childhood imprints, spicy poetic wordplay endowed with meaning...a writer who composes symphonies of words and dances along the cosmic plot lines she is detecting. This is heralding a new style of life where the old story is no longer valid, the narrative of warmongers and suppression coming to an end. A new story is revealed paradoxically containing and rebirthing ancient wisdom. A re-story-ing of how the grand web of the universe is entangled with our personal lives boiling down to that marvelous gem that tells us all living beings matter to the grand web. The whole journey is a wake-up call: what you do matters and impacts the cosmos . . . Creation is a creative act and we are all involved. Read this book as an eye-opener, I-opener, beyond the eye/I. Join the dance of *Space Encounters III*!"
—Chris Van de Velde, Light "Looper," Zen practitioner, Belgium

Space Encounters I

"For the tour de force it implied—pioneering, as far as I am concerned, some sort of very bold typographic decisions—this seems to be a great leap forward from Margaret Harrell's previous books. Last night, or just the night before, I reread this volume entirely. Meaning I again substituted for the "ideal reader," god bless him, and tried to figure out more than I ever have before. And it worked. It thoroughly and convincingly "clicked." The stuff—debatable or not, for any nonsuperficial, committed reader—is in there."
—From the Publisher's Desk, Didi-Ionel Cenuser, Shakespearean scholar, author, Romania

Space Encounters II

"Margaret Harrell has the most open-ended and far-reaching mind of anyone I know."
—Rhea A. White, the late Director Exceptional Human Experience Network

Praise for the *Keep This Quiet!* Series

Selected Review Snippets

Keep This Quiet! III, rev. ed.—*Beyond 3-D*

"Margaret Ann Harrell's book of initiations is a golden bough, a sacred marriage, an initiation, a wake, a book of revelation, a literary and spiritual journey into and through an ever expanding universal consciousness. Margaret Ann Harrell's BEYOND 3-D is her Big Book, her epic narrative poetic masterpiece.

"Brilliant as a literary and psychoanalytic and spiritual text, it is a deeply touching and vulnerable human story. A book that breaks new ground by combining and weaving together such a broad spectrum of genres. I congratulate her on having the courage to write the book and share the book with the world."
　　　　　　　—Ron Whitehead, Lifetime US Beat Poet Laureate

"I am amazed and in awe that Margaret describes these principles *through* real-life experiences. Incredible . . ."
　　　　　　　—Jef Crab, Taiji Master, Taoist, Rainforest activist

ISBN (hardcover): 979-8-9904800-1-8
ISBN (softcover): 979-8-9904800-2-5

Cover artwork: Grant Goodwine, https://grantgoodwine.com
Cover and interior design: Deborah Perdue, https://illuminationgraphics.com

A Published in Heaven Series Book

Published in Heaven Books include titles by His Holiness The Dalai Lama, President Jimmy Carter, Thomas Merton, Seamus Heaney, Hunter S. Thompson, Jack Kerouac, Andy Warhol, Allen Ginsberg, Yoko Ono, William S. Burroughs, Edvard Munch, Diane di Prima, Jim Carroll, Amiri Baraka, Gregory Corso, John Updike, Rita Dove, Wendell Berry, David Amram, Douglas Brinkley, BONO, Ron Whitehead, Lawrence Ferlinghetti, and many more.

Published in conjunction with Saeculum University Press of Sibiu, Romania, and Raleigh, North Carolina

For inquiries, signed copies, and speaking requests, contact the author at https://margaretharrell.com

Romanian National Library CIP description:
HARRELL, MARGARET A.
  Space Encounters /Margaret A. Harrell. - Sibiu: Sæculum U.P.S., 2002
  2 vol.; 21 cm
  ISBN 973-99499-6-7
  Vol. 2. - 2002. - 424 p. - ISBN 973-99499-8-3

821.111-4=135.1

Library of Congress control,
  Love in Transition series: 97153772
  Marking Time with Faulkner: 2001272573

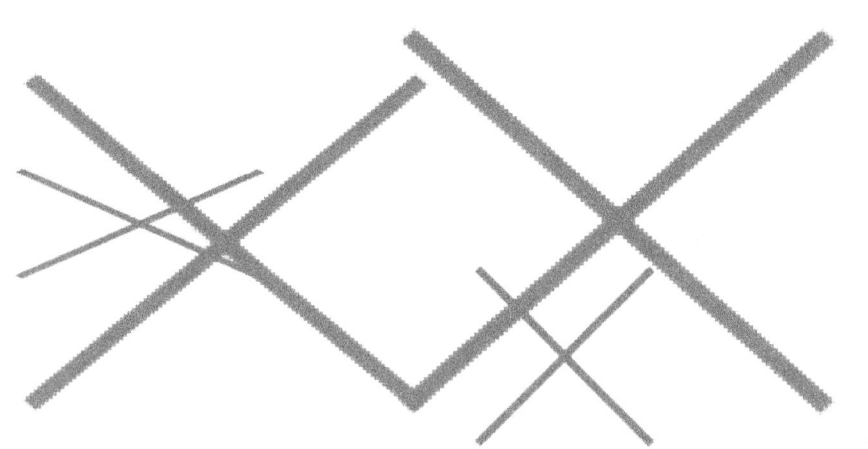

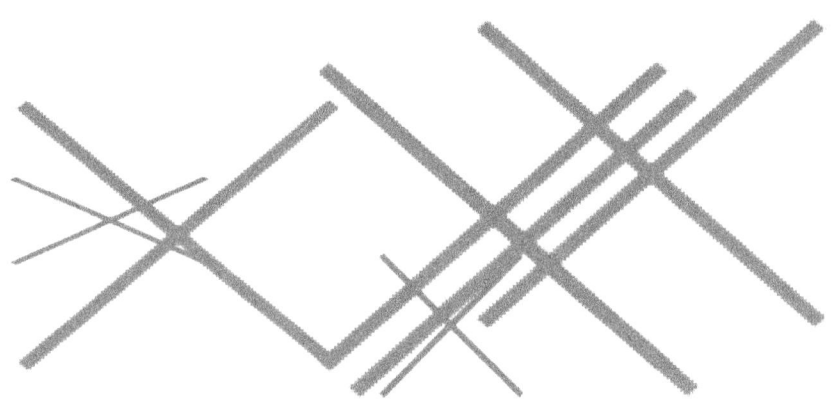

Contents

Author's Note

Newton, when he had all the universe to speculate in (outside time) and was by himself, in a sense (that is, his audience was universal presence), had some different things to say. Things relative to universal interaction and gravity. And fields that related to it.

IIL

For instance, let us look at the effect of the universality OF MIND.

Newton's law of universal gravitation—that is, everything is attracted to everything else: every particle of matter in the whole universe "attracts" each and every particle in it—provided the first clue to the existence of universal connectedness.

Every particle of matter IN THE UNIVERSE was connected to every other particle? He was flabbergasted, astounded. How was it possible? But that's what he said. His discoveries, which we built on for these over three centuries, led him there. And he went. But filled with questions. He left them for us. And that's where this book starts

Why are you, fifty miles from me, yet connected to me in some mysterious way? Can you influence me? Supposedly, yes. "But," sputtered Newton, that admittedly great scientist who would have won a Nobel Prize hands down, had he lived later—who set us down into science for three and half centuries. "But"—he sputtered again—"what is the agent?" Thus, he asked An Underground *PRINCIPIA*'s opening question. He asked it in his own *PRINCIPIA*. We had to go underground, into spirituality, quantum physics, esoteric laws of energy, very subtle energy—pursuing the answer. And did relics of "particles of matter" hang around, holding the intensity of that question? Evidently so, because many picked it up,

How are you connected to "particles" on Venus, on Jupiter, in your front yard, downtown, a celebrity? And does that mean that the universe somehow "connects" its content?" Wraps the life force together somehow? And even a flower, a germ, a stone—that connects to you too? What is this mighty agent of connection? We start here, assured that we can never be totally isolated, any of us, not with these slivers of connectedness inherent in us, in our environment, in Life. Thanks, wise Newton. We like this idea in this century.

> *Nature to [Newton] was an open book, whose letters he could read without effort.*
>
> —*Einstein*

⁂

But wait. Did he not also speculate about *repulsive* action at a distance?

Let me answer that.

Who are you?

Newton steps up.

Of course I did. Don't you know that occurred to me too? But I was already too baffled by <u>attractive</u> action at a distance through an agent that had <u>no name</u>, <u>no description</u>. How could I further baffle the scientists of my day by getting into entanglement <u>without the name</u>? "Repulsion at a distance"?

So you wrote nothing about it?

Oh no. I wrote about it. Don't think I didn't. So I wrote paragraphs and cut them out of the Principia

You did. How can I be sure of that?

They survived.

Do tell.

I lie not. I just didn't have a clue to how to explain it. The vast universe . . . I said, I was like a child playing on the seashore. I could only dabble.

And we today feel the same when we think of all the areas in the universe we cannot see.

Is that in this book?

Yes, that too. The dark areas of matter and energy where our eyesight and our most advanced technology cannot see into. We will get to that too. Here, sit while we go into the story.

※

Hello, I'm Jef Crab.

Can I give a little rebuttal from the philosophies of unity, such as shamanism, Taoism, Vedanta, Goethe. With this in mind, as a Taoist scholar and ecologist, I observe that nature is constantly changing.

In the cycle of life (that is, nature) there exists—from the point of view of philosophies of wholeness—no repulsion in itself, *just a flow of movement.* But viewed from the point of view of the flow of nature, all of the aspects of this constant movement, this constant changing—which for me come down to contracting, releasing, interacting—always exist simultaneously.

Superficial observation breaks this great flow down into change / no change. For me, these philosophies of wholeness are the more important sources of information.

Here's just a little note from Einstein: "God does not care about our mathematical difficulties. He integrates empirically."

※

And what of the Alpha–Omega, that unit of time? Where did that come in? Tied to that end? Who did the tying? Did time? Need that tale? Need that time scheme? That point in its prospectus? Its portfolio? Is that what we're working with? In?

Beginnings and endings?

The attraction they had to each other?

Yes, that too, the particles of attraction, following on what we just said.

Holding "the whole" together—in A UNIT.

Why not add them into such a unit?

A *unit of mind?*

Partly.

The Big Bang gave us this principle, of course. In fact, such a principle is intricately involved (one can almost presume, though it is up ahead, and we have to get there) in that elusive unified field that some quantum physicists are searching for. It has to be because what else is Alpha–Omega—field? Yes, field—about except holding "the whole" together? The principle of THE UNIT.

Now, Newton, by his principles, of the external, impersonal gravitation pull, could not say that he might be here speaking about the extension of his laws. He could not because no one would believe him. So he would have to break his laws for the one-on-one attraction, the immobile, fixed world, the reliable one, and speak of the UNRELIABLE world, the one he had not mentioned because he had not discovered it, though his skepticism, his disbelief, about action at a distance hinted at it. This unreliable world, as opposed to the reliable one, would allow him to speak here. And also, it would allow him to be immortal. And also it would allow him to SHIFT HIS POSITION. He was no longer attracted to it. He forgot to say that you could shift your position if a stronger attraction, a more complex opposition, happened to be close by, close enough to get your attention.

Now, Newton was a master of focus. He could stare and stare at an issue, even if he temporarily turned his thoughts away. Why, old Newton was so concentrated he could have held that focus for the nigh-on three centuries since his death (March 20, 1727). Held on right up to here. He could because he knew how to concentrate. Now, suppose this concentration capacity had something to do with attraction. Well, granting, conceding that, why, the very method Newton used, not written down, might have had—must have had—something to do with his discovery of gravity, the pull of the thought—not matter, albeit—the solution, right to his bed while he stared at the question. Because his very method captured, illustrated, and even suggested the law behind this law of Attraction. The internal one, the reason that it was Newton that discovered it.

If I am connected to every other particle of matter in the universe, are all those "influences" some fragments of an "I," and can I make that "fragment" large or small, make it influence me greatly or not at all? Be a "me" to some degree? *OR not at all*? Hmmm. Naturally, these questions that pushed themselves into my mind held my attention. I didn't know why they wanted to be in the book. I had already asked the question in a way. But this was pushing it further. Who am I? had long been a spiritual existential question. And now? *What connections do I have?*

Well, didn't you hear? So many it's beyond our comprehension

Well, what does that *mean*? Didn't I have enough trouble trying to hold my own attention? When now I learn that everything is trying to get my attention or has the potential to. Also, what happens when they lose their matter, recede into time, work their ideas into other minds? Why, the connectedness follows the ideas, I suppose. Quantum-leaps to a new location. Keeping some residue of connection to its old "master"? Well, I suppose, yes. And so, Newton, we welcome you here. Residue or fragment or living particles. Any of that will do.

I am sorry. I have to leave. Faulkner and Newton have been attracted in. And they are busy, explaining how they got here.

Dew-T
Yes, that's exactly it
"An appetite for
Dew"

The Earth wanted to delve into its center, to go into the underground, to use the stock of energy there to fuel its own expansion. But needed protection for that.

11L

"An appetite for dew"—will I ever exhaust these phrases said to me by Milton Klonsky ("we both," he said, "have an appetite for dew")

Plucked from what Earth?
What grass?
What tree?

Also, Newton calculated the VISIBLE outer operations of the invisible gravity. There might be invisible, even internal, operations of this invisible principle. There—

(to be continued)

Author's Note 2

The Alpha–Omega is a frequency. The frequency where as you state a question, the answer is instantly in the frequency and can be heard by the listener, on that frequency. Or if you state a thought, a position, a correction can be *instantly heard* in it.

Through Alpha–Omega you have knowledge, wisdom, streaming straight through your mind, God consciousness. There is no way *not to hear* on that frequency. Thus, there is no way NOT TO KNOW. To "know not" what they do. The action presented, they know, one would say, the response. But that's kinetic.

So if the answer is presented in some other form, that opens up the area where the answer resides. And can be heard. This is the work of the Alpha–Omega.

This is the Christ Consciousness.

A Consciousness as a vibration, where wisdom is in twos: question/answer. Thought/comment on it (analysis, criticism, etc., throwing out the lower vibration).

But in everyday terms, how is it expressed? IS it expressed?

※

Action at a Distance

I recognized an extension of this when I saw a young guru looking at a photograph of faces of devotees who had been into his ashram. He paused over the different eyes, ears, noses, mouths—expressions—transporting energy into them. I saw it. The picture of that moment never left me. *I can do that. So . . . he's shown me a secret. Other people witnessed it. But I don't think they "saw" it.*

I had this tool now. I related it—or do right here—to the other action at a distance, above.

Between the spaces of the distance, from the material object to my mind, between the spaces of the distance of the physical object to my hands, as they moved over the shapes of the waves, that was—

ACTION AT A DISTANCE.

Yes, it was true that if—associated with a manuscript written by me but located a room away, a town perhaps—I found myself working in (as described in previous books) energy impressions in the air, there had to be a "material agent."* I had learned (suddenly bingoed!) this technique.

My body in bed, going over the revisions, my brain was connecting to the manuscript rooms away. That was how all the earlier drafts had been corrected in my first book series, *Love in Transition*. As it was then taught to me in 1985, so long ago I falter to think I could be that old.

The thing that made it possible to "edit" at a distance, which I could do, to "feel" the contours and intensities of the wording, was that the static, at-rest word form had a *corresponding energy form, which had a shape and could be interacted with—by energy of focus, observation, entering-into, momentum. Yes, it was possible to interact* with the static shape. The mind, observing, becoming a part, stilled, perceived—yes, perceived!—the wave or movement state. The state where it was possible to get closer to the MEANING, to forge a connection back to that, to become a more perfect representation, to reenter the pathway to meaning (origin, source, Oneness); step into the communication, BY THAT PATHWAY. But in a shape the hands could recapture, capture for the first time, as the "feel" of the material became clear. I was not reading the words, with my brain, but feeling, with my hands, the "shape" of the energy of the text passages.

Then moving into the room, to the actual "location" of the manuscript, there to work on the "sculpture," as had the mind at a distance. Thus, what was in the "hands" became information, or

---

*"In Newton's correspondence with Richard Bentley, Newton rejected the possibility of remote action, even though he accepted it in the *Principia*. On February 25, 1692/93, in the third letter addressed to Bentley, Newton wrote: 'It is inconceivable that inanimate brute matter should, without the mediation of something else, which is not material, operate upon, and affect other matter without mutual contact; as it must do, if gravitation, in the sense of Epicurus, be essential and inherent in it . . . That gravity should be innate, inherent, and essential to matter, so that one body may act upon another at a distance through a vacuum, without the mediation of anything else, by and through which their action and force may be conveyed from one to another, is to me so great an absurdity, that I believe no man who has in philosophical matters a competent faculty of thinking, can ever fall into it. Gravity must be caused by an agent acting constantly according to certain laws; but whether this agent be material or immaterial, I have left to the consideration of my readers.' " (Nicolae Sfetcu, page 2)

what was in the communication abstractly came down into the layers beneath, and as it was firmly captured beforehand, or in parallel, in this other way, the revisions went quickly.

Another way of putting this: In Taiji class, I went into the movement on a *wave* level, feeling the form of the energy, as it took off *from my hands in the class* and corresponded, on that level, to the *energy shape* of what I was writing, in another location. Corresponded, in wave pattern, wavelength, inside me.

And as my arms and legs and whole body moved, becoming the energy, in clairsentience.

I began reading energy this way in the early days, though it was in my forties, without explanation. These may do for questions. For understanding all that this process and skill, which were activated and already known in me and perhaps are part of my essence (surely are), turned on.

SO IT HAD BEEN!

The principle instilled into me, or that I found myself in the midst of—as the action-at-a-distance form of the book—while I was writing it, used rhythms, songs, question-and-answer, and every other sort of influence inside my mind (put there initially in my Zurich Initiation by a guide) to get me to "feel" the material, patch by patch.

This must be ACTION AT A DISTANCE, the missing link, the missing "piece" that had rebuffed Newton, just as he rebuffed his gravity principle, to the extent it *included action at a distance without further explanation*. No, how could things *exchange information*, or, in a manner of speaking, "influence" other things, without some "etheric" medium? That is, without some medium that satisfactorily explained the situation, he asked.

Well, I wanted to have a try at it, the Question Begged having hung around me for some time. I assumed it had to do with a predisposition. Or with secrets and answers that will make everything clearer. Anyway, that would do, for THIS PAGE.

Author's Note 2002

To return, then, now, to a very advanced initiation I had in Zurich, taking me in great surprise. An initiation introduced in a nutshell in earlier books but brought in here in another nutshell. Suffice it to say that I was convinced, in many external, as well as internal, ways, that some presence, some consciousness, was teaching me.

Then to go to some of what that period, way back in 1985, 1986, introduced. I say "introduced" because it was no more than that. Brief. Perfunctory, in the sense of understanding.

At least, left-brain understanding. Trying to grow into an explanation of it absorbed the next couple of decades—almost. An **early** thing he taught me was about sequence—*what* followed *what* how many times—what "caused" what being often implied; i.e., that tendency was established WHEN A THING WAS FIRST DONE; sequence, once established, even if no one picked up on it, now resided "somewhere"—provided of course that something did not overwhelm it into such a subtlety as no longer to be retrievable. So balancing randomness of sequential numbers or events or gestures was the intersticed memory of connection: that SOMETHING HAD HAPPENED BEFORE.

Gravity, the "star" of the Big Bang, the father of our universe, as it were, was "the first force" to come forth.

> During the Big Bang, a single force called "superforce" disintegrated into gravity and the strong force after about 90 Planck time.
> —Robert Lamb, "How Stuff Works"

If things ALWAYS or OFTEN happened a certain way, and gravity was universal, was it there when they did? Of course. And if so, then, what was its law? What new feature? What about the description of content, as opposed to mere structure?

Universal gravity was *there* wherever we were, or any mass was, or field, with any gravitational wave. So how could it have a cross-sectional or threaded-in relationship *to generic content*? If a mass bent light cones (we will get to light cones in a minute), creating gravitational waves (or, differently put, if gravitons were exchanged), how did that have anything to do with *what was in the mass*, except, of course, that light—when it made us see, as a photon struck our eye—*made us see* SOMETHING.

Now for the definition of "light cones." Lee Smolin, a theoretical physicist at the Perimeter Institute for Theoretical Physics, also on the faculty at the University of Waterloo and in the philosophy department of the University of Toronto, explains:

> The paths of light rays leaving the event define the outer limit of the causal future of an event. They form what we call the future light cone of an event . . . We call it a cone because, if we draw the picture so that space has only two dimensions, . . . it looks like a cone. (*Three Roads to Quantum Gravity*, pages 57–58)

Wikipedia defines a light cone as "the path that a flash of light, emanating from a single event (localized to a single point in space and a single moment in time) and traveling in all directions, would take through spacetime."

⚌

I ask these questions because they "struck me," or perhaps it was photons, carrying the question that did?

If a star followed an orbit, surely that did not relate to content, as opposed to evident warping of space. But let's put aside for a moment the questions on that, and jump. The question of content involved models.

When a model existed, a possibility had happened, become a "fact." On some scales, that duration could be a "flicker." If, as in the accumulation of materials which finally made a planet, it accumulated enough to become a tendency, a probability in certain circumstances, then it was likely to become a statistic. Presence of one thing, in circumstances, governed or probabilized behavior. Response, action.

This unit of action had command orders.

It was free, to the extent that a whole new learning situation could change its response. But then add in the energy laws, pressures, etc.—which filled the atmosphere, where there were, with the other particle clusters, and so on, these tendencies, these habitual leanings, responses.

These invisible "pictures" if we could visualize them, rather than their being invisible codings, as we would probably put it, of information. So they were information which would manifest tendencies or associational probabilities. And they could get to us.

We could pick them up and act them out, as triggers. Invisible triggers which reflected secret (unconscious) structures of our own, which if never having met the energy to activate them, in a formal way, lay dormant.

They were archetypes. But perhaps with short histories. They had accumulations of past interactions, making inbred, but not yet genetic, possibility and probability. Why were they not genetic? Because genes replicated in cell division, a physical expression. *These strings could change faster. They could break up.*

One physical manifestation of a broken path might take fire and incite the rest. They were shortcuts. Shortcuts to CHANGE, FOR US.

How?

Adding it to my personal learning in associational context, I felt I was on to something so big that it took me years and even decades—yes, even half a century—HALF A CENTURY!!!!—to get to THIS DAY.

—which, in what kind of coincidence, mirrors the title of the essay largely sponsoring one aspect of these examinations, "Art & Life"—

But one more non-digression before getting back into the normal "loop" of this series; i.e., the internal, experiential, joined with it.

We do not forget that Descartes pointed out that all things (regardless of form) could be added in the same way, and that Jung, on the other hand, was baffled by the meaning of number; for example, "if a = b and b = c, then a = c"; how could you say that—in that "by definition" he could not imagine a to be b? ("No one could tell me what numbers were, and I was unable even to formulate the question," when studying them in school, *Memories, Dreams, Reflections,* pages 43ff.) And that, of course, before either of these, Pythagoras said all things were numbers.

OTHER VERSION:
Author's Note
Homo electricus

At last, feeling myself up to plunging into the material—no longer just saying that I was going to start—I sat down at my desk. The words started flowing. I felt myself up to, at last, telling the story of what I had learned about electricity and human potential. Further, about how this and the illustrative essay, "Art & Life," mentioned many times before in the *Love in Transition* series, opened a door—and what door—which I have never since stopped walking through.

In the last ten years of consciousness research, I have been assisted and constantly turned around in jolts, shocks, and nudges by the energetic interaction with the printouts in the computer, which respond to and stimulate my brain and challenge the ideas in it, all the while that I sit down to write the books.

The reader will see a montage of works printed from a normal screen, but which turned into a museum of the unconscious, which I was allowed to present to the curious twenty-first-century seekers. Many parts of it built as if standing on a ladder, looking up at the ceiling, constructing bits and pieces into form. Even deconstruction. Presented, then, also to the art world; for that, I believe, is its audience too. And now, the curtain rolls back, this time on a brand-new revision in the series.

It is about a subject that somehow sailed through time, that, mysteriously on the surface, kept winding up in little bits and pieces in different writers' heads. "Art & Life: A Menippean Paean to the Flea; or, Did Dostoevsky Kill Trotsky?"—that's what it was called, this little essay that was to dominate a portion of my life. At least, till I got it done, got it wrapped up. Got the message through.

The message contained the answer to why a subject was able to reappear over and over, in similar terminology, virtually buried in a larger work.

Why, in fact, for instance, I was "grabbed" by an image in Montparnasse, Paris, which began my entire book series. No, I'm not going into the beggar again, but he stood in, as an image—alive, walking around, all the better—making contact dimension to dimension

Why such an "infection," or sense of purpose, could fulfill its mission, take root. And why this led to the point about our "electric"

Nature. How our emotions and mental body, etc., find different intersections if you put them onto the energy level. How transposing the energy down into the physical interpretations and the old pathways may kill a person, while uplifting the meaning and the intersections leads into a whole new hub of the higher mind. How we can avoid what would be mortal if taken down into everyday levels, where the reality is a kind of "acting out"—what could, on the other hand, be uplifted and made into entirely new approaches to life.

NEW VISIONS AND NEW POTENTIALS for humanity—ready-made—can now be pulled off the shelves, put into the carts and taken home to be used.

To underscore how how the printed-out pages of unusually formatted text in this and earlier books were made: they were unprogrammed, spontaneous printouts—not one of which has been altered for this publication, but only put through the scanner and inserted as it originally appeared fresh off the printer, in Belgium in the period of drafting this work, which started in 1997 and came to culmination, in 2002, though picked back up now, in 2024. They might be compared to the paintings of Jackson Pollock, except for the detail of using a computer, and not a brush. Still, the pervasive human unconscious makes itself and its potential present. May 2, 2002

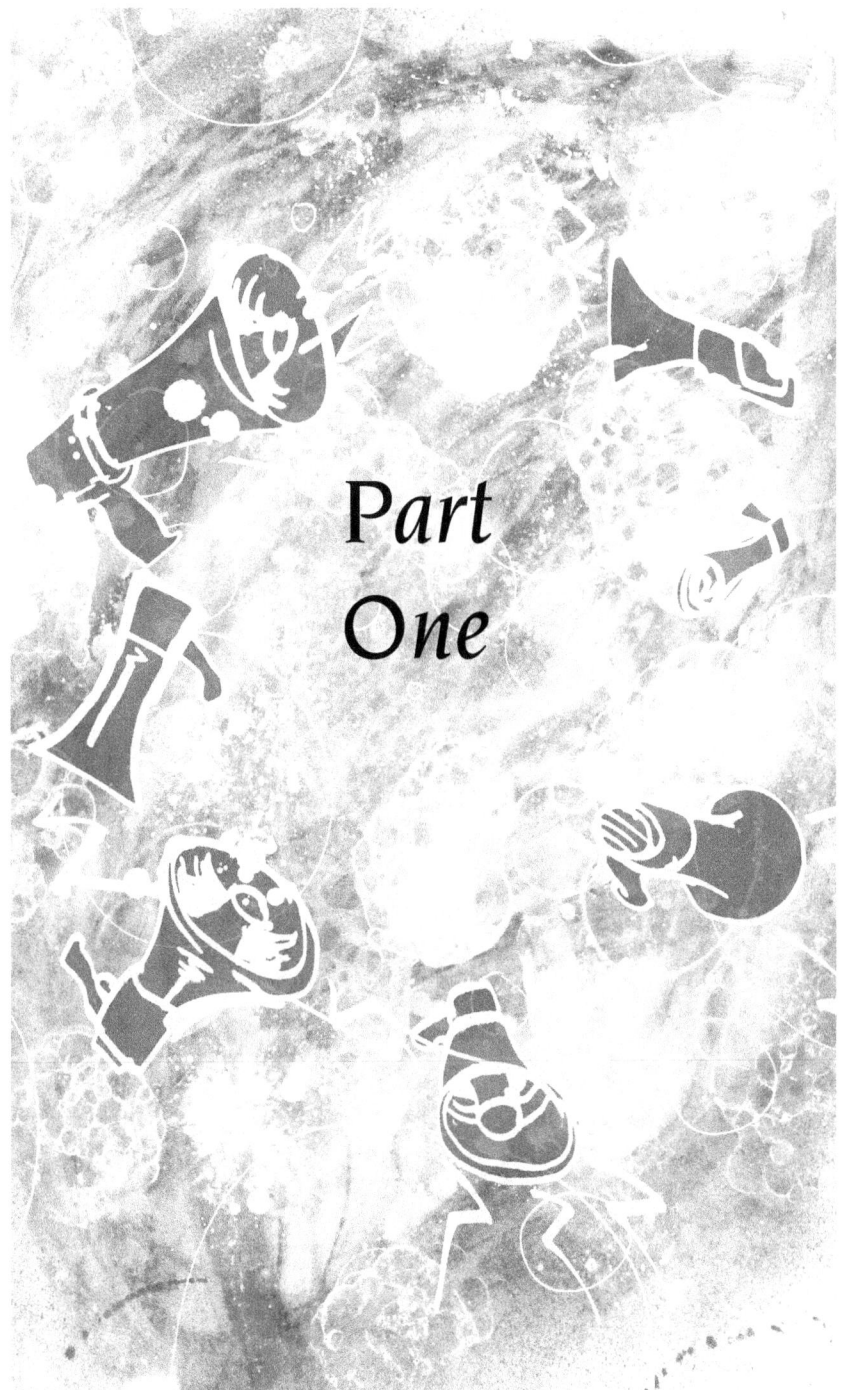

Part
One

CHAPTER ONE

When the Mental Body Discovers
the Abstract Body

Passing through
the Electronic Realm

In "Stilling the Mind for Spiritual Growth," by Shri Anandi Ma (*Shakti*, XVII, No. 6, June 2000), it is explained that going back at least to the *Gita*, by Lord Krishna, to attach the mind to "some divine form or name" is a traditional way of "stilling it." In that tradition, the guru principle depends on the principle of "*Guru tattwa*" (*Shakti*, July 2000, page 7). That is, energy throughout the universe, cosmic energy. In the background of a formless God, which is too refined for many people to relate to, these scriptures provide an interaction with form. A lot has been misunderstood—through not understanding that "the word *Gu* is darkness. The *Ru* is the destroyer of darkness.

On the other hand, this is only the beginning. Page 10, on the relationship between Dhyanyogi-ji and Hanuman—the energy transfers and visions involving his followers—distinguishes between two levels of *siddhis*, or "powers." Dhyanyogi-ji (ibid., 12) speaks of *siddhis* (subtle-energy-based abilities, aka, miracles to the West). He explains that

scriptures and ancient texts instruct ways to tap powers at various levels to acquire *siddhis*. Although it is easier and more immediately effective to tap lower kinds of energies, I am concerned only with the higher levels. I believe that tying into God's boundless energy is the best way. Besides providing *siddhis* for protection and healing, these higher energies will advance you along your spiritual path.

He explains that, by contrast, "those quickly attainable lower-level *siddhis* are *tamasic* [dark] in quality and lead to karmic bondage," aka, to "consequences," on the causal level, which one then has to "unlearn" by seeing the event-producing results. But Vajra and Panjar techniques are sattvic [pure] and lead to liberation." (ibid, 12).

In the beginning of our modern scientific knowledge here in the West, we discovered a gravitational interaction of the moon with the Earth, visible in such effects as on the tides. (Physical tides, anyway.) Then we actually launched a rocket ship that touched down on the lunar surface. But the Hindu theory was also exploring interactions with the moon—with its own line of development. We can read (ibid., 3, Anandi Ma): "On the full moon, it is said there are sixteen types of energies that radiate from the moon. On the full moon in July (the month known as *Asadhi* in the Indian calendar), these sixteen energies are concentrated in the sixteen petals of the *vishuddha* chakra of the teacher, and these are transferred to the disciples. The different energies have different names. They are said to hold the subtle aspects of divine nectar for the upliftment of mankind. On this specific day, the sixteen colors or energies of the moon are radiating in full force; and through the vishuddha chakra of the Guru, they are again intensified and poured forth for disciples."

So, the full moon radiates sixteen types of energies that the guru's consciousness receives and "steps down" to the follower. And subtly, in potential, these energies hold divine nectar for uplifting humanity. How non-Western, mystical. But there it is.

There is an on-going subjective, revelatory archive of observation behind these descriptions. With human launching pads, human transmitters (just like radios and movie projectors), moderators, anchors, funnelers, more universal form, or specific but high-frequency intention—it travels down into the structure that we know here on Earth; i.e., meditation, "glue," channeling of pathways is carried on not only at the quantum structural levels, but also, WE DO IT TOO, inside the whole tissue of humanity,

3

considered collectively.Only by *getting to the consciousness does one* understand and experience the consciousness, to experience the assumptions stemming off from the groundwork as reasonable or the same as fact.

Not so, the West. Which had little training whatsoever in this form of thinking. It was called mystical. No more said. Finish. Wipe hands. It was thought to be nonscientific. And understood. That is, UNTIL WE GOT TO THE ELECTRONS.

One side spoke of influences of the moon; the other likewise, but much more graphically and in detail. One side spoke of the Light. Finally, in this last and the preceding century, the other side cornered it and decided exactly what it was scientifically:

After stars, "Let's go to a smaller distance, say people size, and consider the physics. Gravity keeps us on the planet, but otherwise it is the electromagnetic force that matters. All of our senses come from mechanical and chemical effects based on the electromagnetic force. Sight consists of photons interacting with electrons in our eyes, followed by electrical signals traveling to our brains. Touch begins with pressure affecting cells in the skin, leading to electrical signals propagating to the brain. Hearing starts with air molecules hitting molecules in the eardrum, interacting via electromagnetic forces. Friction . . ." (Gordan Kane, Victor Weisskopf Distinguished University Professor at the University of Michigan and director emeritus at the Leinweber Center for Theoretical Physics, *Supersymmetry*, page 42). AND SO ON.

> *If there is a particle, such as an electron, carrying a charge, then it is impossible to make a consistent quantum theory unless an additional field exists and interacts with that particle.* This additional field *has precisely the properties of the electromagnetic field*, so it can be interpreted as *being* the electromagnetic field. Since the quanta of the electromagnetic field are photons |that is, the tiny pointlike forms or chunks of light, as opposed to waves|, the photon must exist once electrons do . . . Thus, in the Standard Model |mathematical theory of the natural world, involving quarks, leptons, etc.|, the photon is not an extra or separate part of the world, with electrons and photons happening to interact—rather, once the electron exists, so must the photon. The existence of the photon is explained. With the Standard Model |the above explanation| we finally

understand what light is. (page 29, italics partially mine)

Electromagnetic waves carry energy from antennas to our radios and from light bulbs to our eyes. One of the things quantum theory has taught us is that the energy is carried in little chunks (or quanta), photons. Any electric charge sets up an electric field around itself, and when that charge oscillates (say, in an antenna), it radiates the electromagnetic wave or the photons. We have also learned that there is a gravitational field associated with mass, and there are other fields associated with matter—with electrons and other particles. All the particles can be thought of as the quanta of the fields. (19–20)

To know one thing is to know all.

—Dhyanyogi-ji

Of course, I learned this in the Zurich Initiation. Without a context. You couldn't walk out and start applying it. Not until you knew that, true, it applied. BUT in the electronic levels (where added to everything else we were learning, it now began strongly to appear that time itself, events themselves, ALSO could be and were essentially divisible, in their ultimate forms, into little "chunks" of what had happened and would and could, or "discrete," elementary sizes that—we may then hypothesize—one might pick up and move into positions?? Except that these too were ultra-tiny, in scale, far beneath the rippling combinations we were aware of when *inside* EVENTS *composed of them*, organized out of them. Still, could there be TIME MASTERS and impresarios, as well? Once we imbibed and drank deeply from THIS

CLUE? Or had? Had anyone already, on some far side of the Earth, in some consciousness((es)) ALREADY HERE?????)*

---

* The "smallest unit of space" is the Planck length. James R. Riordon, in "Physicists Split Bits of Sound Using Quantum Mechanics" (sciencenews. org), tells us:

> You can't divide the indivisible, unless you use quantum mechanics. Physicists have now turned to quantum effects to split phonons, the smallest bits of sound, researchers report in the June 9 *Science*.
> It's a breakthrough that mirrors the sort of quantum-entanglement-communication-security-bell-test that's typically demonstrated with light or tiny particles like electrons and atoms. The achievement may one day lead to sound-based versions of quantum computers or extremely sensitive measuring devices. For now, it shows that mind-bending quantum weirdness applies to sound as well as it does to light. (James R. Riordon, Physicists split bits of sound using quantum mechanics (sciencenews.org)

AN UNDERGROUND *PRINCIPIA*, we are calling it.*

So we are talking about this thing we can, even, get our hands on, or an instrument to measure it, as it divides and can, then, presumably (as a unit) be moved around (same theory as earlier).
And resonance can be brought in—by the mind, working with the hands. Or can it??? And do these "time units" carry matter (events), etc.? Also, then, are—aren't?—they movable??? But by what or whom? Of course, traveling through or with or in Light. A reasonable theory?

* Naturally this is after the title of the great work of the seventeenth-century scientist Sir Isaac Newton, who gave us the law of gravitation (the constant of gravitation, G). Do we have your permission, Newton? A salute across the "blocks," or "units" of time—these stepping stones we have found and are standing on.

Or: Further Explorations Inward, into the Nature of Man

—into the orders of reality, or of greater light, or greater range of humanly visible light. That is, as we readjust the compass, for the next VOYAGES. These to be SPACE ENCOUNTERS,*

---

* Of course, and surely, the ego was in quite a bind. It had walked outside a natural relationship to its instincts and environment. Acquired predominating experiences of shame and such emotions. Was asked now to walk right up and DIE. Have the head guillotined. BUT was this or was it not another parable become paradigm that might enlighten it? Suppose this approach to its own death were to turn into a Leap of Faith; i.e., as with Abraham—suppose at the last minute, it was told the sacrifice was called off. Suppose, in fact, it was shown the elementary steps back to where it first Got Lost. Suppose it were to be shown how to, in the terms of these descriptions, find itself, a little the worse for wear but still intact in some form, Back in the Garden.

10

or why the statement: "when two or more are joined together, there I am." Why? By what gravity, what bending of light cones? What travel principle???*

Because no event (no information) can travel faster than light, as the theory of general relativity has it, then our universe is a causal universe, explains Lee Smolin. "In particular, no causal effect and no information can travel faster than light . . .

"In our universe we define the causal future of some event to consist of all the events that it could send information to, using light or any other medium." (*Three Roads to Quantum Gravity*, pages 57–58).

This is astounding: "all the events that it could send information to." Think about it. How many events is your thought, your action, "sending information to"? How many events are you HELPING CAUSE? That's what it says right here. Do you believe it? On this level, I do. As in marriage, I take this thought "to have and to hold."

---

*"A massive object such as a star causes the light cones in its vicinity to tip towards it. This has the effect of causing freely falling particles to appear to accelerate towards the object" (Lee Smolin's *Three Roads to Quantum Gravity*, page 60).

> This tilt is . . . often described as the curvature, or distortion of the geometry of space and time . . . As a result, matter tends to fall towards massive objects. This is, of course, another way of talking about the gravitational force. If matter moves around, then waves travel through the causal structure and the light cones oscillate back and forth . . . These are the gravitational waves . . .
>
> So, Einstein's theory of gravity is a theory of causal structure.

Wait a minute. Did anyone get that? Everyone get that? Gravity tells us about cause? As I was saying. That's it! A high-five. A big heads-up. A mazeltof.

It [Einstein's theory of gravity] tells us that the essence of spacetime is causal structure and that the motion of matter is a consequence of alterations in the network of causal relations.

Yes, this UNDERGROUND *PRINCIPIA* stands on that base.

What is left out from the notion of causal structure is any notion of quantity or scale. How many events are contained in the passage of a signal from you to me, when we talk on the telephone? How many events have there been in the whole history of the universe in the past of this particular moment, as you finish reading this sentence? . . .

Again, the implications of this are astounding. Stop and think about it. I did not get it myself when first reading this. Only later did the understanding jump into my mind—as if taking a hatchet and chopping down a door to get into the room of my reality. Smolin continues:

There are two kinds of answers we could give to the question of how many events there are in a particular process. One kind of answer assumes that space and time are continuous. In this case time can be divided arbitrarily finely, and there is no smallest unit of time. (pages 59–61)

We stop here. The modern world considers time to be, in fact, divisible down to the smallest measurable scale, called Planck. And therefore, to come in units.

"A gravitational wave is an oscillation in the directions in which the light cones point in spacetime. Gravitational waves travel at the speed of light." (page 61).

So—yes, theoretical physicist Lee Smolin, of the Perimeter Institute for Theoretical Physics, is saying, as quoted a few pages back, but it bears repeating:

> The paths of light rays leaving the event define the outer limit of the causal future of an event. They form what we call the future light cone of an event . . . We call it a cone because, if we draw the picture so that space has only two dimensions, . . . it looks like a cone." (pages 57–58)

This, he says, is what cause is, in structure—the light paths that fall inside the range of influence of an event, if the information is traveling at light speed or less. What's that again? Forget pushing and shoving and everything Newton said about gravity? Well, at the least, it has to be looked at more closely. Newton peered in.

"In our universe, specifying the paths of all the light rays or, equivalently, drawing the light cones around every event, is a way to describe the structure of all possible causal relations." (page 59, italics added)

Working over some years, like this, I got closer and closer—without knowing it—to what this definition means to the information arriving in an Alpha–Omega structure and whether speed can even be brought in, in such a connotation, because it is speed that is equal (as a container) to all the information that can be brought in, and speed determines whether or not it can be brought in. AND THIS SPEED IS SELECTIVE. Bringing in only what fits, adds, makes a statement, can be included in the resonance, lined up, suddenly explosively CLEAR

In science historian Owen Gingerich ("Let There Be Light," in Ferris, ed.), we find not only the first milli-seconds of Creation, the Big Bang and just after, described as "pure and incredibly energetic light being transformed into matter, and leaving its vestiges behind" (page 379). But also "the final fate of the universe, whether it will expand forever or fall back on itself to a future Big Crunch, was determined," we are informed, "in that opening moment."

In astonishment, one stops. What is this describing but the pattern—presumably almost the very first existent universal pattern—of ALPHA–OMEGA? So this cosmic, primeval pattern of *beginning-end expanding into content* is like a nugget of Life Form,

13

replicating (giving the shape or image of) the First Origins.

Try and penetrate with our limited means the secrets of nature and you will find that, behind all the discernible concatenations, there remains something subtle, intangible, and inexplicable. Veneration for this force beyond anything that we can comprehend is my religion.

—Einstein

Checking back in, with *Science* magazine, February 2006, an update:

Was the big bang really the beginning of time? Or did the universe exist before then? Such a question seemed almost blasphemous only a decades ago. Most cosmologists insisted that it simply made no sense—that to contemplate a time before the big bang was like asking for directions to a place north of the North Pole. But developments in theoretical physics, especially the rise of string theory, have changed their perspective. The pre-bang universe has become the latest frontier of cosmology.

The new willingness to consider what might have happened before the bang is the latest swing of an intellectual pendulum that has rocked back and forth for millennia. (Gabrielle Veneziano)

The Electronic Level

Whoa. Hold on.

"The essence of spacetime is causal"?

When I step down, punching an indentation into the ground, that's adding a track into gravity: a track that, however invisible, because it's in the quantum level, someone else might well walk into! I pull, attract someone else into my footsteps because where I walk is CAUSAL.

Whoa. If I never do another thing but walk down the street, I am leaving tracks to walk in. Or fall into. Cliffs to drop off of if the tracks lead to danger. To someone else. Maybe I can handle them and someone else can't. Or maybe they lead to a pot of gold. For someone else. Whoa.

But another thought came in. *All this content doesn't count, I guess, because waves can't think. Is that what you are saying?*

But remember, we asked about connections in content earlier. Let's keep thinking on it.

Take this article by Matt Strassler: "Most Particles Decay—But Why?"

> Particles aren't just lying around on the floor waiting for us to sweep them up; we've had to build special machines like the Large Hadron Collider to produce, discover and study them. Why is that? Because most of these particles—with the exceptions of the ones out of which we ourselves are made, and a couple of others—fall apart ("decay") into other particles in a tiny fraction of a second. I mean tiny: a millionth of a second is forever. Some of these particles survive only a trillionth of a trillionth of a second, or even less! (You may well wonder how we find such evanescent things!)

And these particles, lasting only a trillionth of a trillionth of a second, our time, don't they have a purpose, every single one of them? Whoa. No?

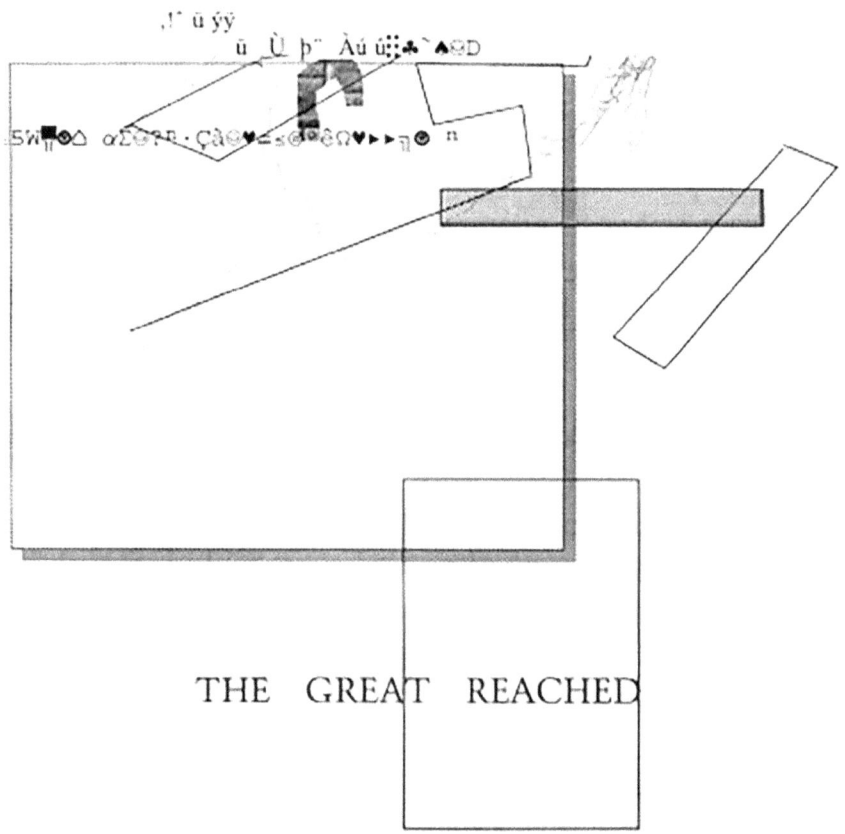

THE GREAT REACHED

Chapter Two

. . . that the essence of spacetime is causal structure and that the motion of matter is a consequence of alterations in the *network* of causal relations. (emphasis added)

Ah-ha. A network.

Let's go on—into a mouthful of a word. But a simple idea.

Invented by Walter M. Elsasser, a *biotonic* law—a mouthful? yes—still not known to Merriam-Webster—"is a principle of nature *not contained in the principles of physics*," according to Wikipedia. Think about it: not contained in the principles of physics! Yet declared to exist.

Wikipedia continues: "Basic to Elsasser's biological thought is the notion of the *great complexity* **of the cell**."

To interrupt, did you know that—to quote Jeffrey A. Goldstein (of Adelphi University)—"*the number of structural arrangements of atoms in a cell is . . . much greater than 10100, a number that is itself much larger than the number of elementary particles in the universe.*"

In view of this great complexity, "Elsasser deduced," Wikipedia tells us, that in "any investigation of a causative chain of events in a biological system," there will be "a 'terminal point,' where the number of possible inputs into the chain will overwhelm the capacity of the scientist to make predictions, even with the most powerful computers." That is, in us—a biological system—there is a tremendous number of inputs into the chain of *what caused what*, we are *so complex*.

Introducing Elsasser's brilliant essay "A form of logic suited for biology," reprinted in *Progress in Theoretical Biology*, volume 6, Goldstein acknowledges how little known the work of Elsasser (1904–1991)— this "German/American physicist turned theoretical biologist"— is, unfortunately, "even though he made important discoveries in several scientific fields and played a key role in introducing the notion of *organized complexity.*"

How surprising that I came across his book *Reflections on a Theory of Organisms* in Brussels, Belgium in the 1990s and lapped it up. Elsasser's life itself was replete with creative twists and turns; it itself illustrates, Goldstein says, a "nonlinear complex system." Moving from atomic physics to theoretical biology with ease, he received numerous awards. In attending the University of Göttingen, he associated quantum physics leading lights, including Max Born, Paul Dirac, Oppenheimer, and also formed lifelong associations with German mathematician child prodigies in abstract mathematics John von Neumann and Norbert Wiener, important in developing cybernetics, information theory, and computer sciences.

Elsasser finished *Reflections on a Theory of Organisms*, with "A Decisive Hypothesis." Let's read a little from that book:

> Previously (in Chapter 3) we had already sketched a distinction between two forms of duplication which we called *replication* and *reproduction* . . .
>
> The existence of the genetic code proves without doubt that the transmission of *some* information is based on the chemical stability of certain molecules. We shall propose the term *homogeneous replication* or, if no ambiguity arises, simply replication for this process.
>
> But in addition we have now an altogether different process that is based on the presumed existence of creative selection [as defined, to qualify it to be a scientific concept] from an immense reservoir of possible states and which we assumed in the beginning of this chapter to occur in such a way that the selected state is closely similar to states already existing in the class. This process will be called *heterogeneous reproduction* or, if no confusion is to be feared, simply reproduction. (pages 68–70)

We will come back to this. It is on point. But, for now, in plain language, genetic reproduction, he says, is not supreme, the only form. He pinpoints another way things reproduce and calls it: "creative selection." No genes allowed. But how? As said, we'll return to this. But lightly. Never fear that it will get too "heavy."

On Time

"How many events," Lee Smolin has asked us—to try to imagine—"are contained in the passage of a signal from you to me, when we talk on the telephone?

"How many . . . have there been in the whole history of the universe in the past of this particular moment, as you finish reading this sentence?" Of course, it is unanswerable, inconceivable.

Facetious though it may sound, *Three Roads to Quantum Gravity* tackles the question, envisioning two different approaches—depending on whether spacetime is continuous (and time can be divided, with no smallest unit, as Newtonian physics assumes):

> But the world is not necessarily like that. The other possibility is that time comes in discrete bits, which can be counted. The answer to the question of how many events are required to transfer a bit of information over a telephone line will then be a finite number. It may be a very large number, but it still will be a finite number. But if space and time consist of events, and the events are *discrete bits that can be counted*, then space and time themselves are not continuous. If this is true, one cannot divide time indefinitely. Eventually we shall come to the elementary events, ones which cannot be further divided and are thus the simplest possible things that can happen. Just as matter is composed of atoms, which can be counted, the history of the universe is constructed from a huge number of elementary events.
>
> What we already know about quantum gravity suggests the second possibility is right . . . The scales of time and distance on which the discrete [divisible, countable] structure of the world becomes manifest is called the *Planck* scale. (pages 60–61, my italics)

Is this all too much for the human brain? In the grand scheme of things, apparently. And thankfully. We will not bang ourselves against the laws governing us and our spacetime. Just bang our heads against our interpretation of "reality." AND we can go at our own pace. Remember, relativity says no two people will "see" the exact same thing, measure time the exact same way, in any given "moment," or spacetime position.

Events do not follow time linearly, locally—are we all clear on that?

Events too did not follow time linarly, loc

$q b \frac{1}{2}$

s too did not follow time linarly, locally.
' had this other location, rhythm. Unfin
-crossed space-time *confinements.* To arri
pact had been *detained* somewhere, in
ı customs PAYMENT requirement, a con
tion, collective, well it looked like—it COL
ΓS WAY OUT. When one continent Ml

For a while, yes.
ished events—lost
ve at some NOW.
 crossing a time
sciousness-raising
JLD BE—that that
[SLAID Aristotle,
n back up, out of
about, through the
ime, which turned
ghold would be in
s before, but that
trance   had some
ppeared, inside a
talizing itself, that

rhythm.　　r|
ents. To　　e/

a time　　a
-raising　　-ı
hat that　　h;
ristotle,　　ri
, *out of*　　,
ugh the　　u
turned　　t
ld be in　　ld
out that　　ou
d some　　d
nside a　　n;
elf, that　　el

In case anyone thinks this is an artist's graphic design, that I sat down and crafted these refocusings of the text, hold it right there.

25

For a while, yes. But they had this other location, rhythm. Unfinished events—lost track of—crossed spacetime *confinements*. To arrive at some NOW. If impact had been *detained* somewhere, in crossing a time barrier, a customs payment requirement, a consciousness-raising precondition, collective, well, it looked like—it could be—that that worked its way out. When one continent MISLAID Aristotle, *centuries later the universe would produce him back up, out of concealment*. Then there was the information retrieved through the Return of the scarab, knocking at a window in time in the twentieth century, albeit that its normal stronghold would be (if to underscore a point the way it did) centuries before. It managed to convey that its precise appearance had some magic meaning to it. Significant to Carl Jung, peering at it, at his window. Then it disappeared, inside a theory, of synchronicity, surviving and again immortalizing itself, that way.

As I've previously explained but elsewhere, they are "computer-PK" images the computer itself independently of my conscious mind "made up"—cutting and splicing and making "pictures" of bits of what sat "normally" on my screen. It has a field day with my text (pun intended).

To me, they adequately and exactly illustrate the text—as well as any cartoonist. Or deep-thinking philosopher. With a carefree—careless? slapdash?—rearrangement of pieces of the whole screen view, they hammered into my head that energy *did not obey the laws of the "screen"* view, but its own laws.

And as it traveled, it *divided things up*.

Anyway, to avoid excess description here, I will continue without going into detail except to add that I considered the letters (such as *bOW)—which always accompanied these rearrangements—like "signatures," each one on a separate printout page far outside the margins, sometimes screeching to a halt hugging the very outermost edge.

Enjoy the pictures, knowing the computer and some beyond-currently-scientific-explanation provided them for my and now your enlightenment, perplexity, and informative quizzes to "explain the workings of," the mechanics in Earth terms. Years later, in taking a course called "You as a Focus of Consciousness," I saw these refocusings in even more clarity. From out of the whole, a piece comes—you, me, all of us. A piece that bears down on a point, an angle—mathematics, as Pythagoras perceived.

This outpouring—and stacking up—of computer-PK pages went on all through the 1990s in my apartment in Tienen, Belgium. Ransacking the area for space to be stored in.

I luxuriated in the "contact" and the artistic (to me) sheafs of paper spilling out of my first pc printer when I pushed "print." Guaranteed, signed, sealed, and delivered, these imps, or divine wielders of physical laws we did not know, were at work whenever I sat down at the computer. AND sometimes even if I didn't. Sometimes I could hear sounds indicating activity even if I was at a distance. HARK. "At a distance." A clue?

In "Contrarian Theological Afterword" to *The Whole Shebang*, best-selling scientific author Timothy Ferris has data on the question "What has been discovered about God?"—from the cosmologist's point of view— and although he answers, "Nothing," he adds something remarkable from Sir Fred Hoyle, about "resonance states" of carbon atoms.

Carbon atoms are made inside stars. To make one takes three helium nuclei. The trick is to get two helium nuclei to stick together until they are struck by a third. It turns out that this feat depends critically on the internal resonances of carbon and oxygen nuclei. Were the carbon resonance level only 4 percent lower, carbon atoms wouldn't form in the first place. Were the oxygen resonance level only half a percent higher, virtually all the carbon would be "scoured out," meaning that it would have combined with helium to form oxygen. No carbon, no us

—we can only exist, you mean, because carbon exists and carbon found a way to exist. Looking around the universe for options, it found—da dum—resonance.

> so our existence depends in some sense on the fine-tuning of these two nuclear resonances. Hoyle says that his atheism—and atheism is, let's face it a faith like any other—was shaken by this discovery . . . [As Hoyle reckoned:] "common sense interpretation of the facts suggests that a superintellect has monkeyed with physics, as well as with chemistry and biology, and that there are no blind forces worth speaking about in nature. The numbers one calculates from the facts seem to me so overwhelming as to put this conclusion almost beyond question." (*The Whole Shebang*, pages 304–305)

Let's repeat that: "a superintellect has *monkeyed* with physics as well as with chemistry and biology."

Ferris, in his compendium, recounts for us the position of those who deny that just because we came to exist God exists. They refute the conclusion. No, they say. There's no proof whatsoever. We are no proof of God: "The larger the universe looms, the sillier it becomes to maintain that it was all put together for us. To posit a human-centered purpose to the heavens smacks of a lamentable humorlessness about the human condition, as Bertrand Russell was quick to point out. 'The believers in Cosmic Purpose make much of our supposed intelligence but their writings make one doubt it,' Russell wrote. 'If I were granted omnipotence, and millions of years to experiment in, I should not think Man much to boast of for all my efforts.'" (pages 305–306)

Ferris goes on:

> Flawed though it may be, the argument from design is more robust than the cosmological and ontological proofs.
>
> The cosmological proof goes back to Aristotle, who held that the existence of motion requires an ultimate source of dynamics, an "unmoved mover"—that is, God. (page 306)

So Newton had not PROVED GOD. We left it at that, sometime back in this series. But the purpose not being here to prove anything, but to lay cards of the Earth discoveries and conscious-ness on the table of discussion for the times ahead, on the table of BRINGING SOME THINGS TO CONCLUSION; to make room for the NEW IDEAS stacked on top of each other, sometimes embroiled like bunches and handfuls of electron fields and resonances or enfolded "news" that we had not studied together and thus not seen THE OBVIOUS; trying to get footholds through the door. Not draw-ing any conclusion here, we continued on, but left Newton in the wings, or in the Underground, as it were, of our dynamics—ready to step forth again if chance allowed, with some perspicacious sword thrusts of observation AND CONCLUSION drawn from there. From the unconscious, our unconscious, where we laid to rest, dis-carded, or just suspended, or did not even look at, MUCH OF THE CONSCIOUSNESS MATERIAL

Here, though circular—but there was much space, much ground, to cover and we only dropped hints, bits of material, collapsed thought, along the route—is where Newton could step back in to join the discussion; sit at the table of the twen-ty-first-century Earth, as it made final decisions about the themes it would grapple with in the years immediately ahead. There was much to whet his appetite. Of course, it had been building for a long time, with many contributors, and had he been there behind the scenes No matter. Let us ask, Will he add that powerful rea-soning power and those, more importantly, flashes of genius? That led to unheard-of, unthought-of but true speculations? Back right into his subject matter, MOTION, where he left off, having—as already written—described laws of motion (of push and shove, by force) and also not been able to ascribe a FINAL CAUSE as a result of it. Now, though this is not our general interest at the moment, IT WAS HIS.

As the cones went forward, one could say that the points they started out from—the past, the originators—contained that future at points yet further than where we often stopped the cone—

—forgetting that it was a moving idea, with a possible, sup-positional expanding lifetime. Not something that ended where we picked it up. *But that, tracing it back to its introducer on the Earth, we found its cone GOING ON.*

Not that, of course, these sub-conclusions of the cone trajec-tory *didn't (sometimes) start something all over. From a new point, of their own.*

So a cone went into the future
A piece of oneself
Powered by one's energy

Inside one's question
one's curiosity
one's creativity
Powering through space, through time,
into its contact position
to its contact
Making
the connection

Now let's get back to a topic dear to my heart that I have brought in peripherally before, but now comes a Big Splash—to finalize what I have to say about it.

※

Beginning in Zurich in 1985, I was taught an unheard-of tool to recognize the signals of energy actively interacting with me on the quantum levels. That is, as if to become a cell, a master cell—to perceive that there was a quantum one-on-one, being triggered, that some part of me I had no control of had made contact, which could be some "stray cell, wandering off the reservation, or the very largest structure in my current personality; i.e., I learned to recognize the signals energy gives. The way it speaks to itself—what the SIGNS are—if communication is existing, information is being passed through us. We being the unconscious dupes, test tubes of its route.

q ½

It is certainly true that, with the rise of the computer, digital representations of all kinds, and electronic communications, the 20th century [and now 21st] has become the age of information. Yet information is generally treated as something passive, i.e., in Information Theory information is a cargo being shipped from sender to receiver.

There are arguments to suggest that information also plays an active role. Vision is a case in point. As signals move from the retina along the optic nerve they meet a flood of information coming down from the visual cortex. This downward flow arises out of the various strategies employed in seeing and has the effect of actively screening, coding, and comparing incoming signals. In this sense our vision is not a passive gathering of information but prehensile, a purposeful activity of information throughout the entire visual system from the muscles around the eyes to the cortex itself.[1]

—F. David Peat, "Active Information"

⬧

I have found the collective me, you might say—correlative to the individual me. The one that is spread out over the universe, in stories and events, and that is always present, only in field form.

I have found that one, Marlow, who has so many experiences, and is directing them, into my mind, of the collective funneled into the personal. I am holding that form and—

The collective facet of the person brings in a different psychology.

Quick as a flash, we race to this new, transpersonal psychology. Having lived in it for so long, I guess I could say I know a lot about it.

The deaths in the story were not the end. They were the

Opening into the

Underground Story.

That's the way I read it.

Chapter Three

Continuing Volume V—Part Three and ½

This is the story of the entry into the Electrical Age with blinders on.

So we start here, in a fairytale

Nothing made sense. It was not the explanation because extremes added not just quantity but subtlety.

Fifty years ago I announced that I was on the way here. I made very sure I would be recognized, upon arrival. I built up great expectation. I have finally landed and encounter my lifetime, in medias res. I do not have time to ask if this is possible or dally with the questions I would have had, had this not been an arrival, inside a lifetime already under way. Thus, I pick up where I started, and the gap of years not counted as myself, in this rendition of who is me and who I am, which does not interest me at all as a waystation. *Not having to introduce myself in other terms*, I merely say—and this sums up the situation to here—that I am the one who planted the memory. Now let us go on.

To interrupt: yes, it is years later and is exactly what I did. The words seemed almost like fantasy when I wrote them in the 1990s. Or, was it I who wrote them, as I didn't exist then? But wrote them as if I existed, as to what would happen IF I did—what the possibility, the percentage of chance, was that I could exist. And so, reading as if in a blur, the focusing through veils of time, back to then, up to now, I see that I was merely describing from the perspective of Now, 2024, what tact, what approach, would get me here, when "I" was just a hypothetical to the me writing then. I was writing "off the top of my head"—listening. To whom or what? I didn't know. Didn't care. The words came. Driven. Fascinating to me. I didn't care if they were literal or science fiction. They compelled me, given my notorious interest in going first, finding something new to focus on, to follow. Following, I spent years in the endeavor. And one day, smash, came in for a landing. Which century would it be? Why, I landed here, as predicted.

And God wrought special miracles by the hands of Paul.

So that from his body were brought unto the sick handker-
chiefs or aprons, and the diseases departed from them, and
the evil spirits went out of them.—The Acts, 19, 11–12 KJV.

I didn't leave room for your imagination. I

invented it all already.

—Milton Klonsky

Information is useless
if bartered for
our freedom
of exploration

o, but very many realized it as such

But information (another voice) isn't to explore
Information is entirely
to explore
No, it's facts
No, it is

Space Exploration

From out of the past
An explanation
A motto
about Space Explorations

as a principle
for this new era
OF INFORMATION
Not to leave the energy out
Not to shut it out
in bringing in
the information

So the New Earth prepared its Entry Lines.

Its ENTRY EVENT SITUATIONS.

Chapter Four

GOETHE, vol. 20 (page 138)

The New Britannica Encyclopaedia: Macropaedia, 15th ed.:

And no one has argued more convincingly that the
only way of coping with the inescapable involvement of the
observer in the phenomena to be observed is to let "knowledge of self develop with knowledge of the world."

Such scrupulous awareness of his own mental operations
was, of course, of paramount importance in morphology, the
science Goethe founded and named . . . He did not propose
it as a substitute for the quantitative sciences . . . He was not,
contrary to common belief, opposed to analysis—one of his
favourite maxims was that analysis and synthesis must alternate as naturally as breathing in and breathing out—and his
only objection to physics was its increasing tendency to claim
monopoly of understanding.*

---

* So when Goethe spoke out on—hit on, noticed—this other side of vision, in which, he said, color was a form of organizing information, depending on such things as how much shadow there was, where the Edge
was, he hoped to get recognition as A SCIENTIST for it (lots of luck). The
Edge establishes the image in photography, especially in clouds. We often
ask ourselves where the boundary is, where STOP is. And it's imperative in
sight. Looking up at the sky, the clouds, At a Distance. To find the Edge.

It is this search for Edge—this adding in of edge to a flat scene in a
photo of the sky, re-forming the flatness—that makes what is invisible
able to be seen. Overhead. In the clouds.

In seeking to philosophically investigate "objectivity and reality (more generally) as subjectively lived and experienced," phenomenology, which associates with Rudolf Steiner and others, including Goethe, avoids "assumptions about the external world," Wikipedia explains—it prefers, for its teaching tool, "the lived experiences," aka "phenomena as they appear to the subject."

Prefers to delve into "the universal features of consciousness" through the lived experience? Well, we are with him there. I am.

It sets the ball into our court, for we are living the experiences. A laboratory is not. Not that it doesn't have its place, but is it the sole location of truth-finding? I ask you. Of course, there's also the heads of the people in the laboratory. Ah-ha.

To make sure we got it, he left these words for us:[2]

> The human being, himself, to the extent that he makes use of |—no, *sound* use of—| his senses, is the most exact physical apparatus that can exist.

> Each phenomenon in nature, rightly observed, awakens in us a new organ.

Think of it.

"Out of the practice of science," wrote Arthur Zajonc in *Goethe's Way of Science*, "Goethe saw the possibility of developing new cognitive faculties whose emergence would bring the perception of novel, and hitherto unseen, coherences within nature." He would do this "by staying with the phenomena, varying the conditions of appearance, experimenting with them but holding the phenomena always in view," and the result, he said, would be that "cognitive capacities would arise suited to proper understanding."[3]

> There may be a difference . . . between seeing and seeing . . . The eyes of the spirit have to work in perpetual living connexion with those of the body, for one otherwise risks seeing yet seeing past a thing.
>
> —Goethe

But how not "see past a thing"? How stand still and actually see it? Not to "see past a thing" required, he said, "consistent work."

Goethe sometimes called his method *delicate empiricism* (*zwarteEmpirie*); i.e., "the effort to understand a thing's meaning through prolonged empathic looking and seeing grounded in direct experience."[4]

Filed away in our storehouse of wisdom, here it is: Goethe's advice to us now, even these years later, in the twenty-first century. Telling us to access "the thing *in itself*."

C

※

"*The genius,*" Schopenhauer wrote in his timeless distinction between genius and talent, "*lights on his age like a comet into the paths of the planets, to whose well-regulated and comprehensible arrangement its wholly eccentric course is foreign.*"
—Maria Popova, *The Marginalian*

"Nowhere," Popova continues, "does Blake's singular genius and orientation of spirit shine more brilliantly than in a letter he wrote to a Reverend John Trusler in the summer of 1799, included in *The Portable Blake,* edited by the great Alfred Kazin." In a lively manner she tells the tale: "On August 16, 1799, a clearly aggravated and artistically indignant middle-aged Blake fires back in a letter brimming with the curious coalition undergirding all of his art—vexation with the status quo, deep personal torment, and unassailable creative buoyancy."

To Trusler, "whose offense was great," he writes, the following:

> I find more & more that my style of designing is a species by itself, and in this which I send you have been compelled by my Genius or Angel to follow where he led; if I were to act otherwise it would not fulfill the purpose for which alone I live, which is . . . to renew the lost art of the Greeks.
> . . . I know I begged of you to give me your ideas and promised to build on them; here I counted without my host. I now find my mistake . . .

"In a sentiment, that Tchaikovsky would echo exactly a century later in his lamentation about the paradox of commissioned work and creative freedom," Popova goes on, "Blake argues that what prohibited him from obeying Trusler's demands was the impossibility—nay, the sacrilege—of disobeying the muse."

[I] cannot previously describe in words what I mean to design, for fear I should evaporate the spirit of my invention... And tho' I call them mine, I know that they are not mine, being of the same opinion with Milton when he says that the Muse visits his slumbers and awakes and governs his song when morn purples the East, and being also in the predicament of that prophet who says: "I cannot go beyond the command of the Lord, to speak good or bad" . . .

Some see nature all ridicule and deformity, and by these I shall not regulate my proportions; and some scarce see nature at all. But to the eyes of the man of imagination, nature is imagination itself. As a man is, so he sees . . .

You certainly mistake, when you say that the visions of fancy are not to be found in this world. To me this world is all one continued vision of fancy or imagination, and I feel flattered when I am told so.[5]

To be a Flower,
is profound
Responsibility—

—From "Bloom," Emily Dickinson

"And one of the comforts of [Goethe's] later years was an intimate friendship with the composer K. F. Zelter, whose most brilliant pupil, the young Mendelssohn, afforded him hours of musical delight and deepened his musical understanding."

He had a "neurotic attachment to the doctrine that light is one and indivisible and never to be explained by any theory of particles."[6] (Attempting to prove

Newton wrong).

Hailed by Darwin*

as a forerunner.

The touchstone of Newton's theory was his famous experiment with a prism. A prism breaks a beam of white light into a rainbow of colors, spread across the whole visible spectrum, and Newton realized that those pure colors must be the elementary components that add to produce white. Further, with a leap of insight, he proposed that the colors corresponded to frequencies. He imagined that some vibrating bodies—corpuscles was the antique word—must be producing colors in proportion to the speed of the vibrations. Considering how little evidence supported this notion, it was as unjustifiable as it was brilliant. What is red? To a physicist, it is light radiating in waves between 620 to 800 billionths of a meter long.

Newton's optics proved themselves a thousand times over, while Goethe's treatise on color faded into merciful obscurity. When [mathematical physicist Mitchell] Feigenbaum went looking for it, he discovered that the one copy in Harvard's libraries had been removed.

He finally did track down a copy, and he found that Goethe had actually performed an extraordinary set of experiments in his investigation of colors . . . How does a shadow divide the white into a region of blue and a region of reddish-yellow? *Color is "a degree of darkness,"* Goethe argued, *"allied to shadow."* Above all, in a more modern language, color comes from boundary conditions and singularities.

—James Gleick, *Chaos: Making a New Science*, pages 164–165
(my italics)

Also,

We should try in vain to describe a man's character, but let his acts be collected and an idea of the character will be presented to us . . .

Colors are the deeds of light; its deeds and sufferings: thus considered we may expect from them some explanations respecting light itself.

—*Goethe's Way of Science*, page 19

2. Leonardo da Vinci, vol. 22, pages 955–956:

"Two special features make Leonardo's notes and sketches [beginning to take shape 1490–1495] unusual: his use of mirror writing and the relationship between word and picture.

"Leonard was left-handed; so mirror writing came easily and naturally to him. It should not be looked upon as a secret handwriting. Though somewhat unusual, his script can be read clearly and without difficulty with the help of a mirror—as his contemporaries testified."

Just not by looking over his shoulder.

But the fact that Leonardo used mirror writing throughout, even in his fair copies, drawn up with painstaking calligraphy, forces one to conclude that, although he constantly addressed an imaginary reader in his writings, he never felt the need to achieve easy communication by using conventional handwriting. Yet occasional examples of normal handwriting (drafts of letter, notes, and comments to be submitted to third parties) show that Leonardo was completely at home in it. In the overwhelming majority of his notes in mirror writing, therefore, one gets the strong impression of "monologues in writing." Finally, then, his writings must be interpreted as preliminary stages of works destined for eventual publication, which Leonardo never got around to completing. In a sentence in the margin of one of his late anatomy sketches, he implores his followers to see that his works are printed.

The second unusual feature in Leonardo's writings is the new function given to illustration

vis-à-vis the text. L
language that was clear yet ex
his vocabulary were the result

vis-à-vis the text. Leonardo strove passionately for a
language that was clear yet expressive. The vividness and wealth
of his vocabulary were the result of intense self-

study and represented a significant contribution to the evolution of scientific prose in the Italian vernacular. On the other hand, in his teaching method Leonardo gave precedence to the illustration over the written word; hence, the drawing does not illustrate the text; rather, the text serves to explain the picture. In formulating his own principle of graphic representation—which he himself called *dimostrazione* ("demonstrations")—Leonardo was a precursor of modern scientific illustration.

Thus, during Leonardo's years in Milan the two "action fields"—the artistic and the scientific—developed and shaped his future creativity. It was a kind of "creative dualism," with mutual encouragement but also mutual pressure from each field.[7]

"Let 'knowledge of self develop with knowledge of the world' . . . scrupulous awareness of his own mental operations" . . . "intense self-study" . . . We pocket this singular reminder from two of the greatest geniuses in history, putting it into our pocket—or list, if you prefer—of what our suitcases need to contain.

But who among us has this capacity for developing "knowledge of self"? Anyone with that capacity, step up. Everyone did. The whole world did. It's what we need to learn.

Palimpsest

Time with his old face
Death with his skull face
God with his No Face
Under my own face.
                    —Milton Klonsky

※

The twenty-first century arrived, full of commotion, the twentieth century passing like a locomotive out of it. I realized that the end of the twentieth century, this century just left, was setting its direction for several more centuries. You could tell that, as the twenty-first century began so dramatically—setting up issues and stages (it appeared) far ahead. It was not a flat time, as it were, the beginning of the twenty-first century—but just as if there were an inherent, formal sense that something was BEGINNING. And/or that issues that would come up in the course of its span had to be introduced IN A HURRY. Plunging down onto the Earth, all at the same time.

For instance, suppose the "canopy, as it were," over the Earth, the great overarching determiner of frequency or focus points, had changed without our knowing it. But the planetary consciousness did and was therefore responding in a way that would shift our own attention, to the issues ahead. NOW HERE.

The anticipatory mechanism, like that of a deer when it senses something approaching—suppose that sensing mechanism (or we, in fact do suppose that that sensing mechanism) of the planet, now over-arched by a sense of itself as a planet, moving as one, was AT WORK.

Announcement: Outer to Inner

Did I expect somebody else to do it, and they didn't? And I wind up in this body, in this position, when I should be in another?? It's like I woke up in a lifetime that couldn't be mine. I was angry at parts of myself for having taken this lifetime, and now look, when they had found me, what they had made. Surely they didn't walk to find me and then bring me out and have only this to show.

So he (with a "toe" on the Earth), would come out right in the beginning. He was in the end. But he would start here too. He would walk through the pages with us. Perhaps, then, he would make a difference on *every* page. Who knew? Else, why? Why try to merge what was so different? I had failed him for sure, failed in being given the lifetime and only having this to show. I didn't know why the sense was so strong. I had been given a SOLEMN commission. I had forgotten it. And now here he was. And what had I to say? To show? It was as if this lifetime could be erased, to someone to whom it had little interest. The past far into the past—had suddenly sprung alive, as if there were no distance to cross. The depth of certain stands becoming perfectly natural to me. The discarding of what was not natural to me.

n was
id not
 could
me to
that

I had realized, at last, that th
not exactly myself, because the a
known. By those laws, there wer
come to reside inside a physica
terms with my causal body, sure

ie author of what I had writte
author existed inside laws I hz
e all sorts of ways information
il body. I had also finally co
; that it existed; it had made 1

▲

I had realized, at last, that the author of what I had written was not exactly myself, because the author existed inside laws I had not known. By those laws, there were all sorts of ways information could come to reside inside a physical body. I had also finally come to terms with my causal body, sure that it existed; it had made that abundantly clear.

I stop here and comment. It's as if I made models to step into. Tore off pages of screen plays for myself. Wrote in my imagination, but it was a far-seeing creative force that was in effect. And it was *bringing my life to me. Setting it up.* By imagining these encounters, long ago when they were imaginary, I bid them come. I stood as if with a pole striking the ground, saying, "Bring forth water." Only, I said: *Come, I will be ready. Do not spare me. Make my life count.* To continue with this beseeching of this higher form of me to step in, that I didn't know at the time was a real Call: like standing on a spot in nature and giving a call an animal recognizes, a bird does, this was a call that energy understood. *Quick? Jump into incarnation*, it said. *Oh, wait. You don't need to. She's incarnated. You only need to make contact.*

The discarding, I was saying, of what was irrelevant, the jumping to the higher view. Even frequency. On the edge of normal view—as if something else were there, right off the screen.

Something that made me a bit jittery.

I was not really prepared. As the energy in it had moved from the sense of how much had been done—extraordinarily much—to

HOW MUCH HADN'T.

Aside: Me stepping in: of course, you know I am not really this severe. I do not judge if my personality turns the lifetime on its head and does something entirely unexpected with it. But this is not the plot we are in. Perhaps I speak prematurely.

So he would come out in the open in the life. Playing various roles. From the beginning. Not prejudge. But waiting till I had *what* I had to show. And what had I? Barely a flower cut and put safely into a vase. Barely anything brought TO CONCLUSION. That was it. This was the conclusion I was on my way to. But he was pliable. Couldn't he help out? Because I had finished over and over again and over and over again the ending had been

"Just so. "That much off. That much to the right, and it could have been— I was being judged there, in the totality.

A new pitcher was being sent in. One of those pinch hitters in the top of the ninth. There was still some time. But it would not be me who did it. Everything had been called off. All things "in the works" had been stopped except a couple. Yet the lifetime was needed. Why? It had not stopped any of the patterns that were— outdated. That I was in, in fact. What had it done except "catch me up," with who had in the totality of this entity, spared me this much time—to see how I would do. Well, just **a little bit**, then (thanks for the bold). Let me practice at the car wheel. Let me give the whole thing a whirl. But somebody down there wasn't laughing. There was something that didn't count here. Something that DIDN'T COUNT. NOT A BIT.

And who was it, him or me, that had had these close calls with success? I'm no longer sure as, at this point, having arrived. I cannot recall such failure as is described here—by him or by me. It was on another level, for sure.

So with this prologue beside the other prologues, we will see how many characters are speaking and where the "congress" is taking place. And all of it. The shadow, you see, was the brains behind it.

Shadow? This was as far-fetched as it could get.

But you (I) couldn't know it then, when those fantasy words left my fingers. I do now—you can—which is why my fingers rushed in.

Do you see how, I asked my current self, *writing it back then*, the thoughts going through *your* brain—how that perfectly situated you for the last year or two? How when *the Real "go signal"* came, you ran and ran. And ran. And ran. And are running still. You are a house afire. *Because of setting yourself up to understand the "go signal." And this is it*!

✳

As I concluded Book IV of *Love in Transition* (which none of you has read, because it was published in Romania and my own copies are in my house in storage), a note of **In-Conclusion** broke in. It was not in the material already in the book. But in the desire of the Conclusion itself, to include more. It had information it had not been able to *bring out*.

It struck the note of reserving the right to come back when things were more settled down. (Or even if they were not settled down. And could never settle down.) I was not even sure of all that had been left out. But that some important things had, things that needed introduction if at all with space. And that things that had not happened were already also weighing in.

Thus, walking down the street, I suddenly felt surely the Law of Gravity about Endings. Gravity about when something was to BE CONCLUDED. This law, we will soon go into. It made me understand, however, that if at the Conclusion, when all energy should have been rushing toward Conclusion, it instead stopped and surveyed the area, accepting new material, that there was a reason that the Conclusion was taking a nonstandard shape and scope. It was supposed to feel itself as At the End. Instead, it felt itself bombarded. Why? We had to see. Thus, it was not proper to conclude as if things were all wrapped up.

The end announced that it was

Something that asked for Continuation.

Walking down the street, having urgently to go to the bathroom, I try a trick.

I know it is *no use to hope* that the nearness of the bathroom itself will *not provoke* the urgency into greater extremes. So I imagine to myself that the end is

Ç

stretching, receding into the distance. The square of the distance. I talk myself into this idea, that contrary to normal, each footstep does not take me closer, BUT FURTHER AWAY. I become sure, in a flash, that this is
the law of event gravity.

That a thing soon to be, as the time grows nearer, makes itself FELT by the body. There is a time sense that works like this. The nearer to the time, the greater strength is needed to wait.
Thus, this is the law of gravity for time. Not for physical objects. But for time. The gravity of time. How it adapts to its own lengths. Thus, Beginning, in time, has little gravity. Before Beginning has less. But momentum established, gravity builds.

And thus, near the end, it can almost not be held back.

Against the law of the gravity of the End, thus, this book went into a law of NonEnd. Did it want NOT TO ENTER the Law of the Gravity of the End?
EVIDENTLY.

Newton said he would oversee the journal. Faulkner would oversee narrative passages. We would see what that would produce. We will walk this way. Now. We will.

Gopi Krishna, *Kundalini: The Evolutionary Energy in Man* (pages 206–207):

while seated comfortably on a chair, I had gradually passed off, without becoming aware of it, into a condition of exaltation and self-expansion similar to that which I had experienced on the very first occasion, in December 1937, with the modification that in place of a roaring noise in my ears there was now a cadence like the humming of a swarm of bees, enchanting and melodious, and the encircling glow was replaced by a penetrating silvery radiance, already a feature of my being within and without.

James Gleick, *Genius*, Richard Feynman biography (pages 99–100):

> As its size diminished, the electron's energy grew, just as the pressure transmitted by a carpenter's hammer becomes thousands of pounds per square inch when concentrated at the point of a nail . . .
> In a sense [the hypothesis went] the equations were measuring the effect of the electron's charge on itself, its "self-energy" [i.e., if such a thing could be said to exist, in this simple a statement of it: "self action"]. (page 310)

※

As the body is given up in death of this physical body, detached from the whole structure, so there may come a time when it is the "turn" of the personality.

This was the form change I was learning about. At first, I translated this to mean I was a parenthetical moment inside the lifetimes of a larger whole, parenthetical but "real" to the extent lived deeply.

To be a ?, it was one thing I could dream of, I thought.

※

> And since, in a sense, it is those random fluctuations that lead to the emergence of new forms of order, [Nobel Prize winner Ilya] Prigogine has coined the phrase "order through fluctuations."
> —Fritjof Capra, *The Web of Life*

One would evidently, in such a journey, be inside a consciousness that had some familiarity with this process. The universe within might have many tools that the universe "without" did not know about.

Now the trip, or the experiment, begins: the "downloading" of the kind of consciousness that knows how to travel through the universe within and come out and teach what happened, as a pathway or tool for the twenty-first century to employ.

Yes, I use the term "employ."

From Gleick, *Chaos*, page 71:

> What about the light emitted by matter? At everyday temperatures the light is infrared, its wavelengths too long

to be visible to the eye. At higher temperatures, matter radiates at shorter wavelengths: thus an iron bar heated in a forge glows red, yellow, and white.

These lumps of radiant energy (heat), Max Planck realized, in 1900, presupposed that they were quanta; "that this precisely tuned radiant energy suggested an internal oscillation, a vibration |of molecules in motion| with the resonant tonality of a violin string"; that a "new constant of nature" was these units, "not of energy but of the product of energy and time—the quantity called action."

Things Looked Into—A Chronicle Of

When they asked me to tell this story, you can be sure I almost fainted with the honor. I trained myself to be sure—testing over and over—would I really react, jump with reflex, pull back as if touching fire—if the impurity of the possible interpretations intruded and stopped me. Tried to get to me and put interpretations in the way of the path I was entering through? Yes. I would get sick, nauseated, if not discovered. If I remained interpreted and explained any other way, I would unavoidably do incalculable harm where I was. Where I was entering. It is easier for energy to enter through a human instrument, often, than to be just in the air. It can aim better. Diffuse, and unable to target properly, it might misaim, if just trying the direct approach. So a human vessel is useful, even for something so big as a "cone" of information. I would energetically energize and inhabit—and finally perhaps (but we will see) identify with a physical body.

I was—oh, never mind my past accomplishments, endeavors, successes. Never mind. What matters is that we thought up this solution, of the red-alert warning system, against thoughts that might try their best to prevent me. That is, that would shift the structure to one of vulnerability. For divided, therefore unstable.

Now, as I let myself think and receive these thoughts, it was just as permissive as if I were introducing or inventing a fictional character, which at some point my brain had stopped doing. They had refused to "live inside me." Why? Probably because I had thought fictional characters were inventions and not dimensional possibilities interacting with who their authors were; that is, without a conceptualization of energy put in and TAKEN OUT AGAIN.

Similarly, that characters, put into action in books, stayed there. (I thought.) Other authors, in the fiction vein long enough, who had gifts enough, got to this same proposition in the past, but then they used names for characters instead of, like myself, putting the dynamics squarely down into "consciousness dynamics"—which they were doing as well.

But once I discovered this technique in myself, it was by then too late to call it fiction (virtual, etc.) and work in distancing myself like that. Pure artists and I were doing the same thing (that is to say) when I reached this point. But they worked in declared metaphor, whereas mine might be metaphor, but was, on the surface, literal.

(No matter how many steps removed, the effect could be equivalent. But we will see what is different, in reality, using this supposition.)

Only after exploring that was I allowed free rein again to my "fictional" imagination. But this time, understanding that I was setting forth into LAWS OF ENERGY.

Not into fiction *not* seen as that. I was restricted because I knew the extensions of thought into energy ranges. So at this point, allowing my mind to think through and extend, intuit—*following energy*, I arrived at the present page.

Let myself tell me things through energy pulses, points, hot spots, trails, mergings, revelations, and so forth. Setting me down, trained for it now, right here. In other words, I quieted my ego and let the words (which might well be the Word of God, for that's how one receives it, every single being, from within their own center or information-acquisition areas) speak in their own sentences and forms.

Gleick continues:

> *Clearly—or almost clearly—the brain does not own any direct copies of stuff in the world. There is no library of forms and ideas against which*

to compare the images of perception. Information is stored in a plastic way, allowing fantastic juxtapositions and leaps of imagination. Some chaos exists out there, and the brain seems to have more flexibility than classical physics in finding the order in it.

At the same time, Feigenbaum was thinking about color. One of the minor skirmishes of science in the first years of the nineteenth century was a difference of opinion between Newton's followers in England and Goethe's in Germany over the nature of color. To Newtonian physics, Goethe's ideas were just so much pseudoscientific meandering. Goethe refused to view color as a static quantity, to be measured in a spectrometer and pinned down like a butterfly to cardboard. He argued that color is a matter of perception.[8] "With light poise and counterpoise, Nature oscillates within her prescribed limits," he wrote, "yet thus arise all the varieties and conditions of the phenomena which are presented to us in space and time."

Gleick, *Genius* (Feynman, page 80):

Particles in the atmosphere scatter rays of light almost in the way a gardener scatters seeds or the ocean scatters driftwood. . . The scattering of waves implied a general diffusion, a randomizing of the original directionality. The sky is blue because the molecules of the atmosphere scatter the blue wavelengths more than the others; the blue seems to come from everywhere in the sky. The scattering of particles encouraged a more precise visualization: actual billiard ball collisions and recoils. A single particle could scatter another. Indeed, the scattering of a very few particles would soon become the salient experiment of modern physics.

That clouds scattered sunlight was obvious. Close up, each wavering water droplet must shimmer with light both reflected and refracted, and the passage of the light from one drop to the next must be another kind of diffusion . . . For Feynman the cloud-scattering problem . . . seemed as primitive as any of hundreds of problems set out in his textbooks . . . It came just one step past the question of why we see clouds at all: water molecules scatter light perfectly well when they are floating as vapor, yet the light grows much whiter and more intense when the vapor condenses, because the molecules come so close together that their tiny electric fields resonate in phase with one another to multiply the effect. Feynman tried to understand also what happened to the direction of the scattered light, and he discovered something that he could not believe at first. When the light emerges from the cloud again, caroming off billions of droplets, seemingly smeared to a ubiquitous gray, it actually *retains some memory of its original direction*. One foggy day he looked at a building far away across the river in Boston and saw its outline, faint but still sharp, diminished in contrast but not in focus. He thought: the mathematics worked after all. (emphasis added)

The computer, which through the "spirit committees" (or what-ever else explanation you want to use about my companions in this apartment in Tienen, Belgium) is playing a game with me, as I type, is begrudging me the ability to follow along visually; no, it marks my place on the screen *several letters away from where I am*. I type. There is no way I can see where the letter landed

Then the intrusion intensifies; all I see is blank space. I try to guess how far down the line I am—peering at the blanks, till of a sudden the entire line (as if in invisible ink) pops into view.

Alternately—which just happened—the whole line of letters is suddenly nothing but a tunnel of closing parentheses, with a few letters appearing in the tunnel. I kid you not. The ratcheted-up energy is palpable in the room.

Then suddenly, working backwards from the end, the whole line reveals itself. I am receiving AN

ENERGY TRANSFER

Narrator

Whether the computer will participate now, in 2022, is not moot. It will not. I am on my own, or rather the new Presence of me is.

As I *comment on, decipher, this old text, that it happened to be by me is irrelevant. As I explained, I was that person then, that person zipped into my body or used the isolation to remain there.* But my consciousness had to take these years to catch up.

Well, *so did the Earth too.*

This was perhaps the only way to put that energy into me. And into the page, *where after decades it still remains*—right at this moment. With the untapped-into thoughts that landed with it, still unopened, waiting for me.

Should I interrupt and say: "Message, message—from the Universe before the Big Bang. Hello. I am arrived. I am bringing these—not words—frequencies with me. Streaming them. Not that I carry them, but they come *in my wake.*"

SO I sat and knew why I felt so uprooted again. A memory was trying to take me over, an idea. *Even if it was not a memory, that was the way it would present itself,* so as to impact me with its reality. I had these feelings from somewhere; these feelings were why my heart was feeling impinged upon, almost without hope, it seemed all so futile.

What was it that was futile? I didn't know. But it was a feeling about the size of things, their reduction.

Yet most people were talking about expansions. However, what I connected into was the reduction—somewhere—to feel as if it were gone—when people said it was just arriving, that they felt it, that it was taking them into expanded size. I checked again. No, it was that something was being lost, brought down, made little. So I tried to examine it. WHY did my heart know this thing? What was my heart trying to say????

※

The energy is not in form—*so it can appear from inside*—convincing me that whatever this is is too interesting and powerful to be timid.

I give up. I give up; how dependent I am on the system of SEEING where the letter being typed is.

But my perfectly struck keys, perfectly typed words, look on-screen like this:

which is explained ere y the simpe matter that I cannot see position, but wtch the white spaces; and the marker, the letters disappear—whit spaces,long after ItyAAd them, SUDDENLY become visible. By merelyl confusing th

What if the structure is a point-of-light? No wonder, this way of transferring the awareness, the energy. HOW ELSE????

※

I have newly received THESE QUESTIONS.

TO LIFT THIS SHELL FROM THE Earth. To unenfold it from such a surrounding, like a universe inside a single conception. RECONCEIVE. Release. Take back. Break the bondage. Let the people go free. IF THEY ARE WILLING TO WALK OUT INTO THIS SUNLIGHT. So now, BEGIN~!!!!!

2Q

In a dream, I entered an unused building connected to the level I needed support from now. Inside, I used the energy and left.

I stirred it up, drank from it. It was the "logical" extension, the *implications* of what they had built up. It waited there. "Pure," ideal. I saw that it was not "I" who walked into and *"became" the energy expression of the implications*, but the waiting IMPLICATIONS. And they are still there, but now that they're energized, the inhabitants might be attracted to this level of themselves.

Afterwards, if again manifested from, the invisible presence of *the implications* would be manifested differently. I already had something to manifest. But is this in conjunction with it??? Or are these the non-manifested techniques that *will* facilitate it? I have to find out.

Dream June 2001

> I rent an apartment upstairs, expecting the owner to have no role in my life. However, the landlord wants me to return at 12:00 noon to meet her son. I telephone. A man answers, calling her "Your Honour," referring to something she was responsible for in the building; she could re-create steps through traces of them that still exist; in that way they invented an elevator, but invisible, or subtle—. I wonder if I want to live in a place with this much projected interaction. She has this skill regarding memory and history.

Reading this passage, I take it to be the unmanifested energy, now personified as an apartment I am moving into; a woman in it has a particular skill, *unsuspected by me—to retrace the steps of the past that created an elevator. Subtle, no doubt.* At the time, I was all set to move to the United States in two months; *luckily, the dream/life moves will be correlated—the unmanifested energy* opening from the position I'd reached being compatible with the move.

This mysterious son the woman insisted I meet—i.e., become conscious of—must too carry unmanifested energy (animus, in this case). Now, in conjunction with my next move, there's some unconscious "elevator" on the horizon that, in the past, was built—by her and him. I need to know about it.

She wanted to pass on to me this skill or creation of theirs, of retracing steps to the creation of "this elevator."

The son refers to her as "Your Honour." It must be AN HONOR??????????????? I was happy about the dream, as things seemed to be in place. I did not want my move to involve clutter, insertion of too much work onto my full plate.

<u>2001</u>

Such is the end of a detour . . . But something felt wrong.

I recalled the Initiation in Zurich. Square One. As the spirit guide and I were writing literature together there, he instructed me it had to contain only positive energy. If you know this, it will take only half a page. Bear with me.

Then the consciousness came in—eliminating the negative energy, taking it from each page.

As it (the removed energy) went out, like a kind of "nuclear waste"—these discards of rejected energy in the words, descriptions of conversations, habits that, according to this cosmic spirit guide, had to be removed—it could strike someone like lightning *if vulnerable* to the discards . . . an encounter with "their own karma." It was harmless to most people, but not to someone carrying—and unlearning—that "lesson" that was in the removed energy.

I did not have—nor did the Earth have, at that time—either the position, the authority, the credibility, or the opportunity to make it otherwise. *No one, in fact, would have listened.*

Not then. Now, yes.

I did not go back, sitting like the Buddha on that moment, that instant, that took off, into blazing light—starting at the point of Zurich. Slashing through the detour opportunities. Seeing them from these perspectives, where the insecurity of what could not be anticipated, but waited through, kept calling. Drew me all the way to here, *where I wait for it.* Not then.

So I sit here. I am not anything. I am a little bundle of energy that eliminated all the things that would normally keep it alive, attracting it into experiences. I, or that energy, which I became attracted to and which was not attracted to life—for some reason, which I did not yet know—kept me alive by attraction to it. May 1999.

✳

Sitting in the center of the geometrical design of me, I saw that there were lots of lines filled in. But not this one. THIS one that was now calling all the rest "detour."

But not so if I added in this piece, which "turned the light on" to all the rest.

I, this I, solitarily concerned with staying alive because it had something to FIGURE OUT: the chunks of answers to my secret question. Even the question, I would keep to myself, not telling the reader. That would "take a load off," not to have to. To start as if I didn't even know the question, but would eliminate the headache if just going into the nondetour direction. I would aim straight for it. Set my compass there.

I would have no horizons at all, no predictions as to whether *this* universe or *that* universe existed, no assumptions about how one looked at these things, and from which angle they were explained in that way, or the other.

But just to go straight for it, in the inner sense—that one that knew why the attraction had to be met. I had said I would be there, whether anyone else at all was. That I was sure to be there, so not to call the meeting off. Hold it to its schedule, and I would come. And make sure that whatever the meeting was to be about, and whatever to accomplish, just to go right ahead with it, *because I would come*—everything else being a detour, relative to it. And so we would decide, those there, how much had to be shifted now.

How much to put differently, into the air.

It was a meeting about the twenty-first century, what things would sift down, archetype-wise; be heavy with energy in the unconscious vein. I had been a recipient before. When I shifted my style of attraction to life, on this level— denying every experience offered—then it set me up for redistribution. I was to be, from the position I had been in, redistributed, but then even that principle became shown to be a principle standing in for another. I WAS TO FILTER!!!

A different composition can begin right in what one

thinks is the middle if it turns out that the detour has ended.

So here I am, not as a reporter. Not as anything. A *little chunk of energy, that wanted to know why it has been treated this way—removed from all the structure that it knows, or that its ego knows, put into an unconscious state perhaps. But at what could be the height of the consciousness that it was in, suddenly this blackout as to where it is, relative to something else. Because suddenly the world looks to be in trouble. The world has some problems.* AND THEY ARE NOT EVEN INTERESTING. *They come from just "refusing" to see, from pretending. From hoping, even, but with false hope. Uncoordinated—so it appears from here. Insistence on—*

And so we will go on. Focused on art. Art that, as it always has, looks for something poking up. Something not flatly blended in, something setting itself apart a bit, something where there is a secret, such as *this one. Something that had perhaps for centuries held its breath.* Tried it the other way, hiding in silence, waiting to be called forth. To have the world find that it could not do without it!!

Otherwise, it could just wait. No need to force itself up at the wrong time, to miscalculate and fall back into the fathomless, measureless seas and waves of nothingness, where it had come from—but in this case, from the never-had-been. From the waiting-for-the-first-entry.

So we tell a story that has never been told before, though we ourselves do not yet know what it is. Where it comes from. Except that it has no strictures. It is perfectly free. We have no one else and nothing else to listen to. It has got our attention.

We have no fears of what our readers might say because we have no readers. (We think. Little do we know.) Even if we say, "Dear Reader," and we love that reader. And we also know that in some dimension in fact we do have a reader or many readers. But sitting right here, we do not have them. And we are not bullied and tamed by them, and afraid of them. We are not hostile to them, but we sit in the chunk of energy that is, at the moment, greater than them because—yes, there is a single *because*. Because, on this subject, which we have not gone into, from the precise angle where this chunk of energy exists and only exists here, we are correct. We know more about it than they—otherwise, we would not speak. If we did not exist, we would not know more about it than they. We would all be equals on the matter. But here and here alone, I on this solitary rock, this chunk of energy that has got my ear, it knows. And so I listen. If it is able to find a world that wants to hear of it, perhaps I will instantly find myself there. I do not know. I only know that at this moment of extreme unction almost—of power, but nothing to have power over—I start out in this vein. Which so far led to HERE, though it is always insecure to stop and hold on. Yet it ensures existence, however insecure and even premature.

※

In the great attempts to hammer at and solve a situation right now, we overlook an important fact; as time does not have our "tenses," that very thing we are trying to "solve now" might not be ours at all to solve, but that of a FUTURE SELF, who is being greatly discombobulated by this thrusting and hurling about of an issue that merely needs to lie low. An issue that is not ready, will meet with no welcome, if bothered at this time; we should not be pressed to do anything about it. WE KNOW.

The cellular information, working on something now, may, however, send out right now some of its work, while still in the physical form in the present, thus working in the future because it is the future self that has STARTED ITS WORK. Thus, it will be the work of one lifetime extending itself while it does the work of the next lifetime, to the small or large extent this can be done, as its next self has stirred and begun.

※

The real death was to be avoided.

And at the moment of this shift, as the old is killed, NOT TO LET IT KILL THE NEW.

So I felt the back (or past) taken care of, and the present (or future) emptied, so that only nothingness was there. The nothingness even accompanied itself by periods of shutdown of my body, when the stillness created near-sleep that must have been in a brainwave deeper than theta, but without sleep. At this juncture, the soul deposited information, but directly to the cells. It was the only way.

It was the bardo of the death of the century, the death of the millennium, the death of the concept of individually organized religions, the death of—a multitude of deaths, there at once, snatching outside the narrow restrictions of the single thing it looked for, whose time was up.

※

No, we take the leatherbound book from the shelf, the one we never read. How did we presume to read the lines written invisibly? To interpret. To face the world with it. BUT WE HAVE TO FACE only ourselves.

The self trying to stay alive, to keep itself interested, involved. And so involving itself—we let it—with *whatever it attracted* from that perspective. That mindset. That resistance to all else, that called it *itself* or its work or its namesake. It was that that fell, in the disillusionment. It was that that had not held up, all these spans of years. One went back. Did one have to finally, at last, put into words? Spell it out. Was that because one did not do it at the time? And no one else did?

To their own satisfaction, many times. But to one's own satisfaction, never. Never, because it was *oneself alone—myself alone, in this instance*—that could do that. And so one sat with this chunk of energy that was the remaining attraction, that had found oneself at Death's

I RISE HIGHER AND HIGHER. PICK IT OUT OF THE AIR. THE POINT YET MORE SUBTLE. THE SUBTLEST POINT OF WHAT WAS GOING ON

Door and had said no, do not enter there. Do not go through it. Go this way. I am here, the guard at this point. I know what it is you want to hear.

True or not?—one did not even know. But one was willing to—"give it a whirl."

One year later. Having moved forward, letting this return to the Zurich principles (introduced so cursorily to myself) be the focus for the expanded study of where those principles *came from*. Did they really work? How would we ever know?

Einstein waited decades—so did Pauli for proof of the neutrino's existence; so, for that matter, did Newton, who lived in the century of discovering his theories but not the century of proving them. He did not live the centuries it would take to prove his theory. So we wanted to know where that chain, that statement, of my life purpose,

LED.

2022

And then it is suddenly clear that I am to share my own experiences fearlessly. I had heard about "being distributed." It took forever to realize that it is *just giving up the level one is on, having it redistributed* to the people coming up from behind.

But so high, on this level—with feelings about it. At least, coming from me, there were feelings. Feelings of what the hopes and dreams were, the values. What were the values that were held—the philosophy, the iron-clad virtue—of the HUMAN CHRIST; i.e., our heritage, culled up and called MYSELF?

I will warn the reader that for much of the last years, I

had certain memories that I could not speak of. Had no wish to. They were not mine, and if I made them public (as I did in 2023, in *Beyond 3-D*), it would easily become clear why I left them private. But then, why the flashbacks? the "implants"? Merging? Unknown principles, only hypothesized to even exist.

So I left them out of my biography. But I tell you, I seemed to walk into "magnetic moments."

Not necessary to go into here at any length. What was I doing, going into biographies like a plagiarizer, snipping out memories— as from a storage facility that obviously couldn't exist because they began in personal positions—clicking them into mine? OR some-one did. OR allowed me the privilege of walking into them. Just like opening the door, finding yourself in a familiar place.

Is it like a computer chip?

※

The next block of text I pick out from this 1990s/2001 manuscript is about Sir Isaac Newton, who, by going out into the countryside during the plague, not remaining in London, probably saved his life—to then set Western science down firmly in a particular direction.

Was it even significant—that the very science used to get a spaceship to the moon was founded by a man not yet pure scientist, whose name carried the relic of the Leap of Faith syndrome? That, dropping all its references, there were now two very famous Isaacs in our history, both of them spared?

But it went uncommented on, the very coincidence as stated in the paragraphs above. Spared so that the succeeding centuries could carry his legacy, whose name carried the relic of the Leap of Faith syndrome, or was it pattern? Or frequency. But the one taken in the direction of the meaning of staking everything on faith—on sensing, on believing, on certainty—the other having been spared with no Earth comment. No uproar and commentary. No notice at all, even, given to it, ascribed or pointed out. It just "happened," like a tree falling in a forest where no one was there.

These, then, willed by some Sword of Integration of opposing ideas, into the very "Art & Life" flea essay (don't worry; it's coming) that more than caught the attention of some readers in the 1960s. Yes, that far back.

But still, with no mention of the name "Isaac," carrying the bucket of water only so far—to the fact of Sir Isaac "being spared" by leaving

London for the countryside. Or even if it hadn't been that, the coincidence of his being out of sight during the bubonic plague, where it could not find him, search high and low, as it might. But evidently away from the contagion—contagion, was it? Yes—of not just people but their wavelengths of ideas in the air. No, solitarily, he listened. Heard what idea wanted to come NOW into the Earth.

He created new physics as he used his mathematical discoveries to analyze motion through space and time. He performed experiments to measure gravity's pull, and then began shaping his most famous idea: universal gravitation, the theory that would connect every object in the cosmos to the flight of that famous apple from bough to ground. He also stuck a needle in his own eye as part of his quest to understand how light and lenses work. All that, while secluded on a remote patch of dirt in Lincolnshire. . . .

As his definitive biographer, Richard Westfall, meticulously documented in *Never at Rest*, Newton had begun to think about the most pressing questions in science while still studying for his exams in his rooms at Trinity College during the year before the plague struck.[9]

Think about it or not, solitude in the countryside did spare him from the plague and its conditions were ideal for isolated focus, nonstop, pushing himself to solve the burning questions he went into the countryside with.

Burrowed into time as if one could plant a hole in it. And why not if gravity is powered by dents and shapes and warps?

The theme jumped around through the image. As a matter of fact, just how? Because brains were involved. And what they got inspired by. Not that brains can breathe, inhale the germ, of the idea, that way, though they do need oxygen—but evidently they can take in perpetuated themes. In this manner that we are speaking of, having studied hard and long and finally getting some grip on it. Some handle on it. A spade in the hand that really knows where and how to dig. And when it digs something up, knows just what to do. IS ready for the idea. It has been thoroughly looked for; when found, has a sympathetic location to arrive in.

So I picked up this essay—just as if it held the long-looked-for information buried under the sphinx in Egypt, as if it traveled the surprise pathway that information used. I knew well the importance of it—the chaos theory only simultaneously showing its face: the theory that would have activated it—and that by a quirk it came into these hands as it arrived in this century (fluish with its implications). Exactly as the plague arrived partnered *with* the microscopic (mind you) viewing of the flea, precipitating the seclusion of Newton in the countryside. Now jump the entire pattern a HEAD.

Well, I pondered the possibility. Now I did, not at the time. Is there any chance in the world that such gymnastics as the essay might contain a law demonstrable in it? It might be possible if the theory itself held the framework and structure by which the fabric of the transferal, or transmission, of that pattern, locked into multiple locations, might then need only some force that set it off in this time period. I decided to stake out my post in this area, in the position of witness, or listener, to finalize the completion of the mathematician-Lewis Carroll-inspired Earth tale, in performing some rigamarole whereby we get even more "handles" on the *"space"* *vehicle that patterns might use for their transmissibility and communicability in the mind's eye, or the right brain or the nostrils, or wherever and whyever.* Mind you, we know, for a fact, it indeed does take place. All around. But we didn't—for all the years we *worked up to* THIS PAGE.

Hold it. Hold it. Something's coming in.

& IIL

bC

Part Two

Chapter Five

Finally, decades after-the-fact, it occurs to me to ask why I have the memory, chronicled recently in *Beyond 3-D* (mentioned a few pages back) of Jesus in his last moments—almost last words—on the Cross. That is, everybody has the memory in 3-D. But why do I have it in 4-D, where it is "stored" like a stem cell? Hidden? Waiting? In a nesting ground? Why would I relive those moments, when everyone could just read about them? Was it a notch in the ego's belt? Of course not. It never occurred to me to pursue the memory with this question. Run after it, shouting or quietly putting the thought to it: OK. *But why did you come to me? What am I supposed to do with this?* Rather, I thought of it in hush-hush tones. It was behind a curtain on an altar.

I used to think of things like this as private affairs between me and me. But now that "me" had expanded; perhaps there was more to it. (There always is. Usually there's an "after" the "now" is going toward.) So bear with me if I ask a very obvious question, remembering that it derives from *reliving, once,* this memory—I am not exaggerating; "reliving" is the correct word, though not physically in terms of setting, but yes, ripped out of me, in terms of setting, but yes, in terms of emotion—the instant Jesus uttered his almost-last words on the Cross. What thoughts—or further thoughts—passed through his head? spirit? Did any? I do not say.

But if you die with an instruction on your lips—an instruction to God himself—it has to mean something. Go somewhere. Anyway, I, catching the memory, it can do what it wants to do in my own head. I am at least allowed that. No, actually, in fact, I am not allowed anything. I have to follow my dancing, darting fingers, which want to say this. Who is controlling them? Light, I suppose. Assume. Yes, light wants to say this. And it has just as much right to speak as these imaginary (to me) *I's.* When you get to the moment of "Father, forgive them, for they KNOW NOT what they do," agonized and loud, or soft, in historic proportions that fit it, it is one thing.

But what do you do (apply what prescription) if that is not the nearly last spoken word? But rather, the utterance put down. *back up. What's the next sentence?*

I was sent to "tell" something. But not even a whisper of the instruction was put to my ears. I didn't know what I had to say—for a long time. And you would never know it either, me being invisible, not making any waves, so to speak.

What is your contribution, and what chalice shall you place upon the altar of life? Why not this self-same light? Why not claim the highest frequency you can and translate it . . . manifest it . . . The fleeing of self from bondage is very much like being chained to a wall in a cave . . . with this exception: each one who is chained possesses the key to unlock those chains. Why, you might ask, do they not do so? They know not.

And so we leave you with these words from the Master: *Many knew Me not, and for this I ask that our Father forgive them, for they knew not and, therefore, knew not what they did. Could you fill the chalice which you shall place upon the altar of life with knowledge for those who cannot see, who have not hearing in their spirit, whose eyes are closed or dimmed by darkness? This would be a good work, and I am with you in it.*

—Lama Sing reading for me through Al Miner, April 2000

Is that clear enough for you?

No, it was not clear at all to me. It didn't sound like a very unusual mission, in any case. Wasn't everyone to do that??

But now, in 2023, I see just how unusual it is. For now, right now, I *am equipped for it*. It exactly matches what I am equipped for. It was meaningless, de-energized, generic—before I got this ability to exactly tell them—wherever they are—who "know not what they do." That's my assignment. Straight from the horse's mouth in a reading I trust immensely.

They simply do not know. Have no way to. Through no fault of their own?

Well, that's exaggerating a bit. But understandably, quite understandably in this day and age. And don't forget their background. They lack information they need. Wisdom. Consciousness. *That would turn their life around.*

Holding onto this question, finding in it a seed of humanity, of its potential—yes, trite as it may have sounded some time ago. That's the card on the table.

But here's one more clue in that same session, from Al Miner/ Lama Sing. I had been blessed, he said, to be taught by Shem—. And what did Shem teach? Well, first, he spoke of a chalice. And he taught not to "follow another's tune." Way back, centuries and centuries earlier, I was being instructed in that, a lesson many people still have not learned. Will they ever? If not, they will be put in situations that make the choice stark:

> You were one of those blessed enough to be instructed by Shem . . . You cannot follow the tune of another's song if you deny your own song in the process. If you do, your soul will rebel, for you taught this long ago. Notice each time you have, there has been some force which abruptly or strongly moved you away.

Which explains (to me) why God told Dhyanyogi-ji, in a near-death experience. he had to come back to Earth—not leave right then—he could not "die with any unfinished business." Not that time. Ah-ha. I detect a "law" behind "unfinished business." Another one we don't know? Patrolling our skies, unseen, unfactored in? I include the question marks, but it seems obvious that's the case.

I was lucky enough to have this blasted into me centuries before. Blasted as with molten lead, as with fire and lightning, as with inexorable consequences if unad*heare*d to. For it was all about hearing, not reading, back then. Ears were connected closely to the mind. Inner ears as well as outer. Inner in particular. But outer when it came to listening . . . to what was in the air, what nature was saying, what was a-hum in that period—brought by anything, even the breezes. In packages even. Or just a word sufficed.

And what of the other memory given me—just a day before that one? Perhaps a soul record. But whatever it was, I received—rather, encountered, re-encountered, met as if a living soul—*this* instant.

As if an electronic needle were replaying it live and I were the medium it was recorded on. Reprising it

The moment St. Paul was struck down—captured as it happened, as if with the fishnet of his cellmate-to-be, St. Peter.

Struck by the Light, I next experienced—recorded in the surviving, re-entering awareness—one thing: that I need not worry, just struggle to my feet and stand. In the bit of energy that remained for motion, this thought alone hit, the command that seemed to come from me but in the awareness: Stand.

Certainly, this would be quite handy in the events later in St. Paul's life. No matter who or what smashed him to the ground—by shipwreck or other catastrophe—he was armed; flattening him down on the ground, it could not be as powerful as this. As all-consuming, convincing. Frightening. Even on the road to the Three Fountains—the beheading waiting—he could call on this moment, pull it out so powerfully that it came all the way through time to me. Was that possible? And how? And why?

The restored segments of time now continued in me. I knew this was nothing to talk about. My cells received them, stepped into them. Or opened up their secrets and shared this one with me. We now, years later, have reached a time inset they were waiting for, and I will thus be able to understand the stamina of it more. Why and how I was allowed—who allowed me—the experience. But, I tell you, they did not age. Came to me in undiminished energy. Unaltered. Recognized all the while as not belonging to me. Not originally. Yet somehow (how?), the energy came to join me. Or I it.

Also, the giant snake that just afterwards burst, erect and strong, out of my mouth—in a vision. Why did it do it? Obviously, to bring the power to stand *in this energy* because what did the cobra signify but Kundalini, the Eastern master energy, transforming what was in its clutches, instantaneous? Kundalini rushing to move the energy internally. I had the awareness. Kundalini internalized, moving all the way through the chakras. It centralized it in my core. It said: *Stand up. You are converted.* To what? *You'll see.* As St. Paul did. *You will be used. You are usable.* You are . . . ? Who knows? *Who cares? Do you?*

Whether or not this barely tapped potential has anything to do with "black energy" is not brought up at all for the moment. Before the Cross, but without an

after," so that there is not that
the archetype *up in a swerve*.
ᴐrgive them. But the next scene
W H A T   I S   I T ?

after." Just there—to take the archetype *up in a swerve*. Father, forgive them. But the next scene SHIFTS. HOW? WHAT IS IT? I must know something about this, as I'm assuming it's the phrase itself—pardon, *the moment itself*—the intensity left in the still-alive lines that speak to us in their energy but reserve some, as in the interior of an unsmashed atom. And in that reserve, they must be wanting to speak. I let them.

Does the phrase roll up its sleeve and show its concealed next step? The potential it was clearly offering us if anyone took the effort to look closely at the words? See that the energy went on? A*h, there. It's beckoning ahead of us, saved till now*, till we enter an Information century, just the visible top of an Information Universe. Top? Well, portion. Clue to.

Little Book

So now I knew how they did it (we will define "they" later).

I had known before, but this is also how they WILL do it. "They," of course, in this case, being the part of "I" "I" call "they."

As once long ago, on a massage table I received a glimpse *of energy entering* me—so did the masseuse. Perhaps as my soul (or whoever it was; speculations up ahead) entered me as I was born (or at least, *a dream afterwards said so*)—perhaps the result of that. The dream referred to has my mother and me trying to walk down a slope together—a slant. As we walked (was it up or down? down, of course; I am trying to picture it)— As we walked it, I saw that my mother turned back because of a male figure—trying to come toward us, in the same narrow area as my mother and I were trying to walk, thinking there was room for both. I've told this story before. But now I have it—rediscovered—in all its trappings, its paraphernalia *of scans*. So I can't but tell it again, letting the energies that made the computer printouts I call PK show off their creations.

I might speculate that the second entry meant that my birth was delayed, maybe just a few contractions, because of this figure who entered—trying to come toward us. I say this, knowing it might be all a metaphor, but what better to describe energy? It was visually "real"—personified—in the dream.

I said, thinking there was room for both. But not my mother. Sh

e stopped our walk,

for that length of time it took for him to go first. I think she was afraid. For me. Because she did see him, in the dream.*
And what was the very first time I saw "him" after that?

I did not see him again for seven years. Then suddenly he was there in my awareness, realizing where he was. I mention this prior-told story here because now I can take it further. And do.

The first time I was aware of the presence of this Omega figure of me was when his alarm, his acute discomfort and incredulity, pierced into my awareness. So great it was that it took me over. And I froze beside a woods, holding my first book of poetry, as his thoughts rang through my head that he was "a great writer," and what had he to do with me, a child? How did he find himself in this absurdity, as if the universe had misplaced him? Mislabeled him. He grappled with the astonishment as I, hearing every thought, "vowed" in that instant to "catch up." And so it went. I had "seen" him, whoever he was and for however long he would be there. He had delivered his message that if he was to hang around, I had better clean up my act. I had "done nothing," he loudly railed. How was it possible? He could not have done "nothing." Not making any allowances for the fact that I was only seven.

---

* I once learned in a workshop, and believe, that—obvious when thought about—the physical birth, the prefiguration, like a map, is a form of a pattern we come in with, acted out. Set up to influence us in later "beginnings."

"See, bring in the pattern," something in us or around us says—with no one holding up a card to say "Remember." Assuming it would be remembered, unconscious. Fortunately, it was *more than that.*

119

I was relieved that I had

something to put the overflow into and not pile it down in foot-notes in the preceding book, which means an emerging structure, something I don't yet know, not the end—but the beginning of something entirely unknown. And that is where the energy comes from and why it is rushing out, so fast because I am meeting here this author, this speaker, for the first time, which for the moment is me, myself in fact— We will see what is happening. I hardly know how to comprehend it, but to start back with myself the infant: impossible without medical breakthroughs. *I could not even be carried full term without doctors, scientists, medicine inventing a special technique—for the benefit of a lot of people, of course, but I was one. Without their assistance, I could not have come to the Earth.*

This "birth," on top of that, signaled in the dream by the sug-gestion that right at the exit out of the womb into the Earth, there was still a question if I would make it. A hesitation. A careful study of the space needed, the situation.

Now with this book begun, perhaps I can stop destroying the other (I will explain that). I see that it is perhaps about my birth again.

Birth patterns repeat. Rorschach test—birth/pattern. And it did not occur to me until sitting here, at my wit's end, wondering how to get back into myself; how to enclose myself again, enclave myself, how to hurl myself behind the "wall of silence")—

As I thought all this, I sat down here to write that I was, at the last page of volume IV of *Love in Transition* (which was so hard to end, that goes on endlessly, in draft, as piles of pages arrived instead of the one last page, indicating a fork in the path; in fact, really the arrival of the series)—back there, before the eruption into *Space Encounters, trying to take my hand and lead me* here.

I now wonder, ask, suppose, say (yes, I sʲ
and started to write (which I have now nᵢ
or confession, the bewildering thought, t
it (to myself at any rate), I had gotten iᵢ
holder of a field that had to be walked th

I now wonder, ask, suppose, say (yes, I say it)— As I sat down here and started to write (which I have now not yet gotten to) the words or confession, the bewildering thought, that I would have to admit it (to myself at any rate), I had gotten into the position of being a holder of a field that had to be walked though (a karma field is one way of putting it, a field of "lessons/opportunities"; and in fact it is probably true that every single person contains some bit of it); that my own karma (activated now) seemed to be combining with others.' Naturally, of course, first daring to speak the thought to myself, I did not know how generic such a situation is. Yet this field seemed to have a warfield component. Why? I am required to rush, seeming to be holding warfields (that is perhaps the job I had been given), but *pattern wars*. Wars between old and new patterns.

And was that what I really was

t to do? **And then I sat**
lear. My birth. This
of birth situation I
ιere there was the
future? anytime? to
alance, settle things

meant to do? And then I sat down, and it all came
clear. My birth. This was the desperate kind
of birth situation I was given—the one
where there was the attempt from the past?
future? anytime? to push time? knock it off-
balance, settle things

0W

now; so that there did not have to be crosses and crucifixions. This me, sitting here, examining, letting it happen. Holding. Not letting go. Letting the body, which had been prepared, knew how, Go Through with it. And then, this idea came. It had been like that before; simultaneously a consciousness entering while my mother turned me back. Turned me back away from the exit. But the contractions had begun. Both met, in the body at the same time. War and death. Life. Life without these old patterns.*

I am going to speculate (this is in April 3000, pardon 2000) that it could be lifted so high up, archetypically speaking, to the level (the rim, the notch) where as one century exited, or one major thought in the consciousness, a new one entered at that time; a leading figure to speak for it did. Did so, in synchronized motion. Therefore, the movement was peaceful, because the two were conjuncted. Maybe I had seen the primitive draft of this, in dreaming what appeared to be the pattern I myself happened to be physically born in. Perhaps it was a century pattern, as there was something peculiar about it. After all, this new century, being born, was a new millennium. Carrying its own concerns. Not that we yet knew. But perhaps they slipped in. Just as in the birth dream I had seen. *Perhaps they slipped in, in tall conscious form.*

---

* I am getting really excited. The *fully evolved* presence—that form. Perhaps it co-entered, precisely with the baby. Waited. Perhaps the evolution was of NOW. Right now. Perhaps the evolved form is trying to activate. And the squeeze is tight. Then and now. Perhaps my mother was right to sense this. For the spacetime that allotted us will have to accommodate us both. Could that be perhaps the source of the terrible pain in the back? Perhaps he enters through the pain. The pain that can be borne. I can bear it. Perhaps that is it. OR not. We will see. For I am here to stay *and sweat or figure* it out.

Only one year later, surviving that, I am asking whether this very scenario HE—the Initiator in Zurich—is in NOW, at this very moment, in trying to take a different step INTO MY LIFE, is the source of THE BLISS, sometimes there, taking me off guard, out of nowhere, the way he used to

So that I, the tiny new upstart creature, a mere baby, did see, at that very moment, the Omega of the same form, that I was, and it (the century) was, in. Saw the whole pattern together. Though the larger figure frightened my mother (in the dream). The thing was, not to get frightened. I had seen the practice "run," the condensation, the sense of a spirit creature, large, staring down (just as in an OBE), in surprise and first view, at the baby, and then entering it (in the dream/vision). Entering it outside my own consciousness, which was viewing this while I identified with my mother and the baby and the project of getting me BORN.

Now, these scores of years later, I was grown up—finding myself in the time scheme of the birth of a millennium, passing out of the millennium that began in 1001. Perhaps it was all taking place, undercover, like that. THE CONTINUATION. The prepared-for architectural slimming and refashioning, remolding, just as a great sculpturer would do. Only, the fabric of our ideas, it would be. Which might be, if you knew how, no harder to mold in THAN STONE.

So the Alpha, perhaps that is all we had seen 2000 years ago. Setting up positions for THE OMEGA. Not that they both weren't there earlier, but that what Alpha initiates as Alpha–Omega, Omega finishes, also as Alpha–Omega. But in a totally different spatial scene.

---

lift me up on a street into his energy, when I was merely walking, DURING THE INITIATION, which we will finally go further into, as we gradually have, in its proper thoroughness OR
ITS DEPTH.

I was—deduced I was—in the pattern of— at the peak of power being struck a blow from behind (I am now re-experiencing it right in the back-shoulder area); we all know that pattern; in fact, I keep pushing it out of my mind, telling my brain not to think like that. And so it does. My next thought is: *But no, it is* NOT *that pattern, because the one who stabs me, or even if it is myself miscalculating, is in* AN ENTIRELY DIFFERENT PATTERN *and moment, or split-second. Time is not at the same tick. Brains are not thinking the same way. The position is not the same. The field is not.* One reason time is different in the two positions is that one of the players faces a different future, another yet another. And this is how my birth arrives, attracting—for it does—a constellation in which people have Days (DAZES, more likely) of decision, or culminating judgment, inevitable in the very conditions of the field I am born in.

0

I walked across the border with it, just as my mother had with me, I, a consciousness, now seeing that what I had held was itself a child, a collective child, and I walked across the border with it, for I was in some way its mother, though in the collective sense it was a Child of the Times. And everyone was its mother. It was all in how you looked at it. So I will tell you how I saw it.

I have walked into my birth, which

ı picks up from my death, and
ıt return to the moment (so I
hen keep going. [&&I attract
[find a way to draw the energy
ening together) and close out
ıat benefit (and not otherwise)
sition to this. &&]

h picks up from my death, and I die in betrayal. To be born, I must return *to the moment* (so I recognize myself, my feelings) and then keep going. [&& I attract repetitions of the agony of that, until I find a way to draw the energy here, hold it (the two actions happening together), and close out outside interaction, or somehow let that benefit (and not otherwise) from the tangential position to this.&&]

rbC

I am trying to explain about the flea and history, about the "pawn" portion of humans, the chessboard of life; about the observer (myself) I have convoked here, so as to have someone to observe and report. To put it into the comic book narrative, and then show how patterns make us pawns.

We will see what is happening. Now with this book begun, perhaps I can stop destroying the other (as said). So I see that it is perhaps about my birth again.*

※

What process "[promotes] the stability of information in heredity"?

Elsasser has dug deep to devise his own answer: *parallel processing.*

Why, the answer, he finds, is—da dum—*two processes, not one*: homogeneous replication *and* heterogeneous reproduction.

"But in order to apply this result, it will be necessary to assume that both these processes are active in the living organism" (page 70). That is, we humans use both.

Whew! And Wow! Now, here comes a radical analysis of holistic processes involving—hold your hat!—mysterious, invisible, non-contained appearances and disappearances, slips of location, that move the information into approximate positions where it can and does—hold your hat!—approximate the form it *used* to have.

It has memory, just like, come to think of it, "when the light emerges from the cloud again, caroming off billions of droplets,... it actually *retains some memory of its original direction,*" we learned from Feynman. The light "remembers."

Now, not only hold your hat. But hold this thought.

He (Elsasser) said to call these processes "regularities," not laws. At least, insofar as he knew at that moment. However, there is a problem with that, as he points out. All through the entire universe,

---

* This is later. A whole year has passed. I am under compression. Like a lid is on top, and underneath a volcano. I am aware that I am under compression, and if I say a word about anything, it decompresses and a fountain spews out. The information will hardly stop pouring. As is the natural state of compression when you take the lid off. Then I am likely to not know when to stop, find myself begin to wobble, with the amount of information spurting out. Like after a wrist is slashed, which is not at all what happened. The lifeblood spurts out. It is unstoppable. What has happened to me?

I am ENTERING A NEW PERIOD.

A different sort of energy. I pass through the out-of-control, or unstopped and unsuppressed, using no judgment, or listening—letting

inorganic matter, like rocks, metals, obeys the laws of homogeneity.

All over the universe, the properties repeat, or replicate themselves. Make copies of. BUT—every single human, in the minutiae of the individual, is different: in chemistry, person-to-person; in anatomy, etc. Well, hold that thought too. We speed away now but will return, to click the underlying hypothesis into our data. Essay, rather, volume, or even entire life and all it included, so as to arrive RIGHT HERE!! that has kept us pursuing its meaning—its message—for nigh on, now, twenty-six years. But this will become clear. Why it took so long to properly pin down and label what its content (human content, in fact) REALLY implied. Demonstrated—OK. Obviously did that as the very vehicle of communication via the verbal level.

---

the outspurt govern. Then it stops and recesses. And I can let it stay recessed. Perhaps it is the time to go back to the Cave style. But what has happened is that I have GOT PAST AN ARCHETYPE!!

The blood rushes to my head. ALL OF IT. PAST. We are past the archetype. Aren't we??

A bread KNIFE (in the presence of Jung) spontaneously broke in two. The bread of the beggar (beginning this series). Let us stop and hold on, see where the archetype took us.

Birth = pattern = what?

Now, I have figured out that the "I," what we could call a "master" draftsman, planner, human being, is in the future. I am characteristically ahead of the times. *Yet* the interval of relationship (interval of separation) stays the same. It is not that I go into the future and am *finally concurrent*. No, rather, it is always the same interval. Like a mathematical formula, where to find me, in any century. Or was, until I figured it out.

Wherever the future is, if I am in it, up to this time, our relationship (the charted path that we have of intersection) is

C

that I am always ahead of what I, in the past, which is the present, *needed* to be present (that is, gain recognition, "fit in" nicely, perhaps even become a "household name").

So much for me.

But what is this?

※

Hanging on the ethers of nothing, then, to try to go ahead, leaving behind—in one fell swoop—this so sturdy frame that humanity has sculpted its plots on? No. We take up the "exclusion principle." We go ahead, minus this one prevailing past inclusion.

Love then continues its development—it expands.

Is it possible it has reorganized—left out the impediment it had so grown used to?

flung it out. Labeled it the Judas in this story.

The prior attachment of guilt to itself.

It walked free. It wanted to see if we (if any) could follow in its steps.

But what kind of new epic path is this

to introduce the ether falsely identified earlier
discarded
we have detected yet another
supposed ether

or Love did
while no one seemed to observe,
it proposed, said
that an ether of disharmony
"read into" its wavelengths
was called guilt
Out, out, it said.

Who would abolish it? AND WHAT TO SUBSTITUTE that was so consciousness-supportive? Responsibility-producing. Did any have an antidote? Did any know how to restructure, leaving such a concept out? What would the emotions do? the understanding of Love? Without the component? But one stepped up. Love stepped up. Saying it was clearly the time to introduce this: LOVE WITHOUT GUILT.

As the world tried to weave its way onto a desirable path,
flung into the universes of stardust, to recombine yet another way
this old concept
it was recycled
rather than
make love recycle
itself

the whole pathway
of the Earth
threatened
the ellipse itself recycling
as in this dimension of itself moving forward
effortlessly
freed of the old baggage
that said it must carry this suitcase throughout eternity, while it
said
NOT SO

Part
Three

Chapter Six

A Universe play
Now I get it
I tried once to write a play
to try my hand at it
The universe listened
Now stepped in with
Its own play, assigning the roles, as after all
We are, it has been said,
But players on the Earth stage
"merely," with "entrances and exits"
You don't say.

It earlier tried epics
Now why not openly walk in and say it was casting
A Universe play
stepped in with the "players"
the actors
on this stage where
We are
The plot
layers

Break, cut, halt. Stage director coming in. We must jump out of this. Get on with the story.

Schrödinger, when he was offering a concocted crazy *what-if*—just as an illustration, a thought experiment—hypothesized a cat that would not be either completely alive or completely dead inside a box *till* the box was opened. Well, it is like that, in a certain dimension of consciousness.

So long as the end, or the situation, is in suspense, and the cells (the organs too, the eyes, the brain) do not have confirmation, then the "real" explanation is still left open. It can be worked with.

Take, for instance, that time when I was aware of the approaching death of Milton Klonsky, receiving all sorts of signals. But then—as I hesitated to telephone, to fly there—in the final moments of not being able to stand not the suspense, but the now-growing pain, he went to the hospital. It all became drawn then—the plan, the events, what-would-follow-what next. But as this also sent signals over to me, I stopped hesitating. Wham. Smash. I did not phone, giving him the chance to tell me, "I think I am dying." And I to say, well, what would I have said: "Don't, until I get there." Or "Don't. I'll get there." Which, instead of in person, I therefore reported to myself in a dream. Followed the story, like a bounding ball, every night—not crediting the reality, only the symbols; he was just fine; life wasn't symbols. It didn't dance through a landscape, pop into reality, a *fait accompli*, having existed in parallel. But since it was quite clear to my artist self, my spirit, what was going on continents away—well, out with the scalpel. I killed him off—the character based on him.

Then against what the doctors expected, Milton, the real one, was immediately going to die, as if following my character. But that wasn't it. I was receiving my intuitive information, outside the time frame of his hospital bed. The character died ONLY because my dreams alerted me of the probability that Milton, the source of the character, was on the "chopping block." Had been pointed out to Death as a likely next target—

—giving my second protagonist, based on me, the chance to express how *she* felt about it, the devastation she could not communicate to me so long as it was "only a dream warning." *Nothing to see here.* After all (I didn't know), he had lung cancer weighing on his heart. Hmm.

In this way, it was—let us say easier—from that dimension, where particle reality processes, as potential, did in fact offer solutions here, to intercept and shift what (if it followed the tract lines of a physical-reality event) would go one way: by physical-reality laws that we know.

And what would, if intercepted from laws and options (that is to say, *looming potential*) of another dimension—the cloudburst of a single option not having occurred—create an entirely different outcome, version, unfolding, overridden future, etc., etc.

And so these two dimensions of law were interacting, demonstrating and telling me not to doubt—to run—that this information was real. Of course, he had to die to prove the point. And if I had *not* learned it in the instance above, I could still learn it—actually, I *had* learned it—

—and *in this instance* if a part of me entered from the time of this much pain, *it was with the intention of ignoring it. Walking right past it.* Then affirming to me how the mind was stronger than matter in these things.

Do not ask who is writing here, or why it first deposited itself in the lower level of this book, underground and undercover, beneath the top text (now moved to the surface), in that I am, without focus *on questions such as why*, merely recording what then streams through. From where?

I myself am always a bit ahead of the times, as I said. Yet the relationship stays the same. Wherever the future is, if I am in it, up to this time, our relationship (intersection) is that I am always a bit apart, awry, disjuncted—not fitting like a peg into a peg hole, but ahead, because of my nature (I have to confess) and also, however, exactly because that is the way I relate to time. A fatal flaw. However, the way to avoid the flaw, the solution I had discovered, would be if I (you, anyone in this predicament, when it was no longer ideal, in any way) came from the future. Ahead of time in the sense of what I relate to, only in the future am I able to fit those bits in.* Obviously. So I miss the missing part of me, that knows better how to deal with the situation—thus completing the field

---

* I quickly hasten to strike down the radical impression this statement might bring, because coming "from the future" means only a radically different organization of the present. Turning "latent" and "unconscious" and "unfinished" and "yes" or "no" into exactly their opposite (or at least conjuncted differently) IN THE VERY SAME PLACE. That will do for a start, of a more complicated explanation. I found this out, in a dramatic way, on the massage table but a few short months before.

bC, &11L

"equation.""*

---

* Let me also explain that we start here by degrees of "I" presence. That is, even though I feel quite sure that "I" is the appropriate word, I might be exploring an "I" that I have never known. That I merely document, but though it could be called Sam or Jon or Belinda, *if in fiction*, somehow it also in this experiment feels equally correct to use the appellation "I."

There had come a time when in the manner described above I stopped using fiction. Now, it does not feel necessarily personal. Merely correct. Equally, I have finally understood that when looking back into our past, if a type of action feels *foreign enough*, it may be that we are, for all "intents and purposes," *not truly that person*. Where that person is, I have not yet brought up to myself. But rather than fictionalize, I evidently decided to take responsibility for all the projected aspects that could have been fictional characters. I somehow knew, or learned—before it became known—the law according to which THIS WAS THE ONLY CORRECT (or preferred) APPROACH. FOR ME.

I see that I anticipated the law I was about to discover. From the pure and true present, looking back and looking ahead is alien territory. That is, the projected and imaginary is just as close to the present as "I" was and will be as those other *territories of the* "I." Again, this anticipates, I see now, the law I was on the trail of. Even hunkered down, sniffing out of its hiding places. Its rabbit holes and other unknown burrows and concealed trick doors.

I did not know the field equation, *of where I am now* and what the field is, because of some particle law, *which I did not know.* But I did in the future. *

---

* Feynman: Why not just eliminate the field? he asked. Like (it had been asked): why not just eliminate ether (in the Western sense of it); eliminate all background upon which things move (in spacetime); leave them to move through *nothing*, so they will be *relative to* nothing, or rather, relative to each other.

Wheeler's wild ideas always contained components that were spectacularly wrong and unworkable, but often contained a kernel of deep truth that would pave the road to an understanding that was otherwise unachievable. The idea of a path integral, the essential tool used to calculate physical observables in quantum field theory, came about from Wheeler's insistence on a sum over histories, but it was Feynman who worked out the details correctly, and applied them properly to our physical Universe. (Richard Feynman And John Wheeler Revolutionized Time, Reality, And Our Quantum Universe (forbes.com)

This, we are told. "It is not impossible for the ink molecules, randomly drifting about, someday to reorganize themselves into a droplet. It is just hopelessly improbable. In Feynman and [John Archibald] Wheeler's universe, the same kind of improbability guaranteed the direction of time by ensuring disorder in the absorber" (Glick on Feynman, 1941, page 119).

Now, remember an "absorber" can be you and me. We are just not equipped for time travel. Why not?

The present authors [Feynman and Wheeler] believe that all physical phenomena are microscopically reversible, and that, therefore, all apparently irreversible phenomena are solely macroscopically irreversible.)

The "macroscopic," by the way, means us. For, as we all know, we are not microscopic.

But in the future, I do not turn back and see what I would have done, had I known it. I am not even aware of what I did in the past. *Not till now.* The scene is one place. My curiosity is at work. But I am

---

SO? Do we believe it? Or believe another speculation—fascinating, this one—appreciate? In fine detail? that IF a light shines 100,000,000 years ago, *perhaps it is because something anticipates it will someday find a recipient?* Well, that's how far-OUT the speculations got, when imagining how our universe functions, based on the new physics.

"The sun would not radiate if it were alone in space and no other bodies could absorb its radiation . . . If for example I observed through my telescope yesterday evening that star . . . 100 light years away, then not only did I know that the light which it allowed to reach my eye was emitted 100 years ago, but also the star or individual atoms of it knew already 100 years ago that I, who then did not even exist, would view it yesterday evening at such and such a time."— H. Tetrode, a German physicist, 1922, in *Genius*, page 120

I do not say all scientists believe this. *Far from it.* This paper by H. Tetrode was read and pondered over, by Einstein and others, however.

It doesn't take a genius to ask some of these questions, and we are not necessarily taking sides. In this instance.

not **present.**

This solution of jumping from the future, with the tasks solved, into the me who hasn't the skills for solving the tasks of the scene (still being created, invisible, not with enough distance for measurement) seemed reasonable. So I try it.

This is my birth. How? How is such a thing possible?

Maybe it's not. But let's give it a try.

Frankly, I do not know if such a thing is possible. Remember, it's a consciousness jump. A consciousness packet. A consciousness field. Not time travel in a spaceship.

And suppose someone heard Feynman or John Wheeler speculate, "just eliminate the field." And where would I be then? In a field that got eliminated right under my toes?

I am, like always, trying to figure out WHERE I am—relative to which "I *don't know what.*" I finally realized that it is impossible to ask my question, even, because it is RELATIVE TO NOTHING. *Where am I?* is not the effective question, but RELATIVE TO WHAT SCALE? I am sitting, desperately, trying to get through the question, confident it has a reason to appear to me like this. For surely the end of my life could not be something totally unbuilt up to. Divergent.

Perhaps, indeed it is the very companion of that moment—of the universe *trying to come onto my eyelids.* I dare not forbid it. For where would I be then, I who am always trying to establish where I am? I will do something worthy of whatever it is that is sending this energy. Bombarding it, raining it down. Realizing that it may not always hit the target. I myself sit here like the

Little Dot that I once experienced myself go away on a journey with—details forgotten, of course (more on that up ahead, for whoever did not get introduced to it earlier), with nary a budge from side to side, nary a move away—I will walk out. And it is this energy I will carry. And the world will turn upside down, for it does not know what has hit it.

So stopping this narrative, I get explicit. It is in this way I settled on marching out of the *archetype* of the Cross.

By going through it, in a way that there was a solution beyond even that of the Cross. Let me quickly add I am not the only one doing this. It is sprinkled around. But I am doing it my own way.

But this solution required skills from the future, which knew how to overturn archetypes like moneychangers at temples. (—I stop myself, reading this for the first time in decades. It's a little bit crazy, I grant you. I cannot stop, with my imagination soaring, whoever is speaking. I am too absorbed in the information. Too interested. Invested.) In view of such an objective, however many of them tried to meet and stop this, with all kinds of patterns that they loosed in swarms like gnats. That they filled the air with, so that no one could see and would surely walk into at least one. And then what? That was where the skill from the future came in. A kind of X-ray ability that diagnosed the situation nonstop. Which, detrimentally, in talk translated sometimes to deluges and downloads (not meant to be where they landed). No matter. That (in fact and rightly named) high-speed energy was fatal if set wrong, it went so fast. Before you knew what had happened, even the most logical person could find himself or herself in the most illogical situations.

Now it would meet the situations, not just with something ahead of time, not knowing how to fit in. But it would, in the narrowest way possible, make ME, at last, at ease in the times. Or, let's say, pull the threads and corners of Time onto my timeline in a "local" sense, here and now. And you can try this too.

No, not anyone can imagine how difficult this might be for a person, because their very own nature would be conceivably unknown. Their habits, everything, except fierily or flashily instrumental in causing situations. OR getting mercurially out of them. What I mean was that I had to discover myself. This was inside me now, but no longer me. It was a guest, invited, a *me* who might or might not stay. But was

in some way inside me, from the future, with skills that were useful and of exceptional perfection for now. Only, on the other hand,
and if misused, deadly. But it now seemed I, looking for someone
who *knew* (as we all might and often do) had accidentally found (as
we all might) myself (or some energy who came, bearing only one
name, "I," as if it were the only, or first, word it knew how to put
into me, the only association

or translation of the energy)*

It seemed that at times—that is, when the energy was set loose (a dynamics was "in play")—I knew the skill of giving up everything, to remain neutral; thus appearing involved in one way or another, while a pattern, a dynamics, started to function, and perhaps even to rage. And just when no one knew the way out, a skill was to keep the focus.

If one managed, if one dared imagine that there was some point where some secret resided in each of the participants in a given situation (whether or not they had ever met and no matter how spread out they were, or even how close), then high up there somehow the communication was made—or there was a chance it would be—unconsciously into the consciousness of each one. No one moved. Everyone was frozen. The consciousness came from a very high level.

This was all I knew about it, except it seemed to have something to do with my twisted shoulder as the way out of myself, in a high-level secret task of making an appearance right now, at the *time it could be most used*. Which of course meant I had to die. Not literally, of course. *Bardo*, death, in order to make use of the future's self-knowledge. Now I am holding tight to the idea here. I am not moving one whit, one way or the other.

---

* Now, when one "finds" oneself, one does not say that "this is good" or "bad." One is where distance stops, feelings are known and there is no question what to do—feel them. One does not have to ask FOR PERMISSION, even if explaining, outside, WOULD BE DIFFICULT. One sits tight AND LISTENS.

It felt, almost, like being in a private world, where I had MY OWN ANSWERS to even public questions. A*nd wherever this world was, it was where I merged with myself.* And for a short moment, it felt eternal. It felt like finally having answers that WOULD LAST, however short the time period they existed in. It felt like something the Akasha would WRITE DOWN for me to read in the "future" and recognize, however another might react TO THIS SAME MATERIAL. These things I recorded as what I "knew." Just say, for it comes here into mind, like that journal I once wrote of, imagining, that existed out on a ledge and had been left for me—that time. Or by me.

Part
Four

Chapter Seven

We had not known how to measure or find interactions where an unconscious "program" was "received" IF it was kept inactive at the time. How to measure unconscious-to-us quantum "registering"?

The fact that something was unconscious would move the consciousness of it INTO THE ELECTRICITY. Where the information was. Stored there. But probably not for long.

Beginning in Zurich in 1985, I was taught to recognize whenever my energy is actively interacting on the quantum level; i.e., being "drawn from," joined to, plugged into, conversed with even (in which case it may or

may not be
inverting (a
halted, *doi*
"signaling."
electricity. 1
it has no
through, ex
place the *c*

come projected onto someone or something else), or is
ippearing as its opposite)—in being unconscious—I am
ng no matter what. What then occurs? A kind of
I feel the tingling, even the determined movement, of the
It is, from that point of view, unconscious of me, because
medium (just like the DNA), on this level, to react
cept—if inside the human "carrier." Depending on the
urrent is—hands, legs, right side, left side—in my body, I
1ation. *Depending on what is going on about me,* I have
;, a quantum picture of the *metaphorical or structural*
1t. I know the dynamics. I had to know it. I have learned
for some time. Not knowing the human, down on these
:tro-magnetic levels,

may not become projected onto someone or something else), or is inverting (a positive attraction appearing to be the opposite)—in being unconscious—I am halted, *doing no matter what.* What then occurs? I feel the tingling, even the determined movement, of the electricity. It is from that point of view unconscious of me, except recognizing my attention to it—because it has no medium (does it?). Well, nothing to screen it for incorrect information—true or false?—on this level, to react through, except if inside the human "carrier." Depending on the place the *current* is—hands, legs, right side, left side—in my body, I have information. *Depending on what is going on about me,* I have pictorial correlates, a quantum code or map for the metaphorical or structural environment. I know the dynamics. I had to know it. I have learned through it—for some time. Not knowing our human susceptibility, down on these minute electromagnetic levels, we build the

Earth karma—the one about to leave, to be dramatically overturned—there.

Channeling electricity: the unconscious can program itself with the TV, as it were, hooking in.

Or let's put it this way: it can "tape" a scene in a program if it likes it—to replay it in its own life. No kidding.

How long could we hide from the fact that "so we have electrical circuits in our brain, our body, electrical impulses—electricity is our 'message carrier.'" Did we think they would not recognize sister electricity out there in the universe or in its very viewing moment at, for instance, the television set? That someone writing away at a plot in an isolated room might multiply this vision just by putting it through an electrical medium? No? Oh, my dears, yes. Storing the electrical nature of the decision, it waits then for the moment the electrical decision comes into my life. Your life. *To* life. If you see that I am stirred up about this, it's true. It made a great impression on me because I did not learn it through reading, but through experiencing it long ago in Zurich, sitting in my studio apartment, my arms wrapped around my knees, as the electricity went through my hands. The body can PROGRAM ITSELF with the TV scene, as it were, hooking in, transferring the intensity as intention, storing the electrical nature of the decision, waiting then for the moment to spring. It has set up an encounter between itself and the borrowed memory. It is a comparison, a consultation, an acting out vicariously. It has shared information. Shared it with this TV situation. It has shared it inside the electrical responses passed in the air between the picture on the tube and the storage units in its brain. It has gathered the energy of determination in this form. The determinant is an UNCONSCIOUS persistence, a knowing, unconscious of the source. It knows what the result will be because it was acted out, as in a dream. Only, the "dream" information was on the TV, and the scene itself was transposed into the human recognition cells. They saw and had affinity. Intensely attracted. It was this abstract, nonhuman-inspired information organization that was picked up. Of plot. And put into the brain cells as tomorrow's agenda.

Yes, that is how it is. That is who we are, temporarily. Trailing clouds of glory, we forgot all this. We see now the images on-screen, not just in the air. When they were in the air, left-over or being-used energies of others, we did not understand how we "saw" them and recombined and stored. Here, to anyone who has had this experience (I wager to guess we all have, unbeknownst to us) of a transfer of electricity from the TV set into the self, and the resulting termination of the transfer. The unconscious-passing implying unconscious support. In this case, it is not even real support, but support in the consciousness. It is the consciousness that saw what might turn out. And the communication between the two sides of the brain is undertaken in this form. An electrical communication of a plot through a picture in a TV set! And the words to it. One now "sees" on-screen what the other side feels and which it was unconscious of. Desires can be communicated, swift as a lark, in this form.

No sooner seen on the screen than electrically communicating: *let's do it. Let's try this out.*

It is something like a simulation lab for the part of the brain that sees it as that—as information, a situation, acted out before its eyes, that it learns from or identifies with or stands distanced from—as if it had magically commanded Life to put its unconscious thoughts into action, seen, however, to the conscious mind as a fantasy situation. Something of a holodeck experiment, brought to it as intensity.

For instance, I feel the electricity in my vibrating hand or leg at the first impact, watching the TV—or perhaps it's a medium I'm unaware of, maybe with no physical technology involved.

Yes. The next day, usually, when the electrical *pattern* returns—if it is negative, felt in my case in the left hand or leg—I try valiantly to forestall it in the only manner I know: by stopping the vibrating.

But have you ever tried to stop electrical momentum? And it has here A GOAL.

In the unconscious, the playback, the impact is what it is stored in.

The perhaps-projection begins (that's in the case of negative replaying of the scene). The scene may, looking quite different but with unconscious parallels, tie into the electricity bingo of the TV scene the day before—that's right; it is working "outside time"—it was tagged as "the same." Now whatever other party is involved enters the high-acceleration excitement/emotion and anything else that this intensifier brings.

We have no idea, in general, I believe/observe, that it is possible to channel the electricity, but think that its computer program settles its pathway and usage: *it goes where it is told to and stays where it is supposed to.*

But the mere fact of the electrical re-creation of a scene on a tube, on a glass front, carries with it far other implications. *To the quantum level, which sees this, there is a possibility of interacting. The viewer can see the situation and derive information. Human beings, then, in such instances, feed themselves this electricity (with information in it, electrical plots, scenes) that their subtle forms could use.*

And that can drug them if this information remains a vicarious playout. Or if they see themselves in the situation, along with the courage and instinctive response, that is transferred instead. It can be a collective transfer, unconscious and unmeant, unprocessed for this kind of effect. It can be. Or could.

If we are using this vicarious teacher unconsciously, we will soon enough be faced with the ethics of electricity. And had better understand what we are dealing with. Learn to incorporate the eventualities.

✳

Where did it wait during the intervening hours after "setting up"? before unfolding? That is, after making the connection, the awareness of likeness, but delayed in setting it down in an action—in that particular person's life; that is, your life—where did it hesitate, pause, wait? Somewhere unconscious from the perspective of the unwitting person, who would now repeat the setup; at which time it might emerge as if apparently *instant* gratification, a perhaps-reckless urge, a "lack of impulse control," everyone said—electrical at that—i.e., seeming spontaneous, electrically so. Obviously.

The electrical experience would announce, or warn, be the moment of the energy's gathering itself—before the physical-reality result, already expressing the supposed attraction, the supposed verdict. Right or wrong. It could be anticipated, avoided, transformed. There was a secret to learn. A built-in solution, or new step; a match of target to intention. We did not need to always lag behind as beneficiaries or guinea pigs, dupes, as the case may be.

L

※

Why was the TV often on *the scene* as sparks flew nearby or "lightning" struck? Here, at so important a finding, we divert this volume!!!—having found the way into the structure. We forgot nothing. Prepared the Announcement. It was a privilege of the First Magnitude.

So we start out into this idea, hurrying and running because the twenty-first century had begun. AND it didn't know this. This was a major discovery in it if one looked back at humans. What they could do—what was *being done* to them. To us.

Up there, hearing the news that the century had begun, HOW I Ran. So as to be given credit for
MY OWN WORK.

(s2Q

Over and over something kept recurring. Something not picked up and made a law of. But it became increasingly obvious that it *was* a law. It had to be discovered.

Take a plug in a wall socket. Everyone can see where the cord is, the socket is. But walk into a room that *feels* electrified. Can you necessarily "see" what is happening? Who is doing what? Not when everything has been transformed, put into electrical mode. Sometimes the "plug," as it were, is easily visible. Sometimes not at all. The training to do so being *in short shrift*. To see the marks (of the trade).

Our brains know how to read patterns. Is it any surprise? Don't they always "translate" to us the nature of the reality they tell us is "there"? The colors, everything? Don't they read: BEFORE we read?

Hours, days might go by. There be no electrical pickup. We are talking in this case of visual situations in which we humans "organize" issues—that these are electrically self-reproducing. In this way, contagious? N*ot possible*. N*ot to us, we all knew*. That it was NOT POSSIBLE we could be made so susceptible. Not possible to be sitting ducks and dupes of electricity. Why, the human ruled this planet. No such situation could happen to them. Wouldn't they have discovered such a law, an interaction—HAD IT EXISTED? Thinking of all the fabulous discoveries that existed.

But electricity knew better. It could "read" our unconscious desires in this manner, stumbling on them with the innocent-est of intents. It was merely taking a walk in the park, as it were, performing a role that mechanically allowed movies into your home. But the electricity did not stay in the wires. It went up into The Story. The electricity knew better—as did the mind. What matter whether it was mediated and passed through the electrical structure of the universe; or disembodied and broken down into code and reassembled? We could not "follow." We "gave up." But the mind—didn't it, rather, "read" emotional packages through the conglomerate in the TV image *that would be displaced later*?

We had our vehicles—cars and whatnot. Wasn't more intangible communication likely to have its own forms of transport? That is, we were "reading" on two levels at once. Deciding ON BOTH. This pattern, once it got set into the public presentation, as organizing instrument, in the electrical mode, was "loose." But one had to resonate with it if to hook up with the *transmission* of "effect." Thus, the transmitted form "reproduced."

This is an almost scandalous situation. But obviously it has only run rampant for a few decades. In every industrialized country it works like this. We can easily be excused that we did not know about it.

So now I have rolled back one curtain on what it took years to reveal: what happened (really was initiated not just into me, but onto the Earth, by the mighty consciousness that intercepted and remolded my life, in 1985, which I can now gratefully acknowledge—becoming the first of the Teachers of the Earth that I would like to use my last decades to bring some people in contact with). Had I not gotten this far, I don't know how this material would have arrived here, though arrive it would have.

Let us now be methodical in studying the situation.

※

Flies—carry germs. Fleas do. Ho-hum. Yes—we all know Nothing new.

But what of inanimate *processes*? Those engaged in subatomic principles of interaction? N*o danger there.* Don't try to tell me there is. Well, what if they carry, just like submarines, subatomic patterns. And jump the scale.

To us. Is it any surprise, in fact, to find micro-mechanisms embedded in macro-patterns here? No one has shown us yet how this works.

Leaving us blind on these scales.
slipping the shackles of responsibility totally out of sight.
Leaving the
unimpeded, *uninstructed* unconscious operations—in a wider
unsurveyed and unpatrolled range. In these open

spaces of the
buffalo West
scalable, are they?

171

These quantum
Billy the Kids
Wyatt Earps
Gunslingers
High noons of the cells

In quantum terms, *cause* of this type (when it reaches our ears)
is without reason or explanation.
going on undetected

All the while, coming from the
opposite direction, the world is being compressed into smaller
and
smaller scales of which *cause* affects—in its repercussions—
the whole
Earth.

Do you think it fair? I did not. I thought the world, if it knew, might
quite easily be UP IN ARMS.

✳

For years, the ego had suffered in silence, not knowing how it
had "cut off its left hand," in developing its right. No more would
this situation subsist. The ego had earned A BOON; i.e., in cutting
off its access to the effects of quantum interaction as registered
by instinct, it had handicapped itself to such an extent that most
advisers urged its death. Death of Ego was the prescription for the
Next Step of Humanity. BUT what about if the Ego were, in gener-
osity, granted by the East A BOON?
But could it be done? Do such things exist? It has been HINTED

TO US that they do.

If you're wondering how I know all this, by the way, I don't. But my right brain watches and "knows" the information is correct. However, it doesn't "know" the information. "I" do. Whoever "I" is. At that moment. It "knows." It dictates, or rather, controls my fingers, whoever "my" is. Oh, "I" am "my," the one in this physical body. But if asked to discuss what I've just written, my mind might go blank. A dud. I don't know this. Know nothing at all. Of this, that is.

So I don't suppose the right brain is even storing this. It's using live "cavalcades." The word jumps in. A procession. Just not a cortège.

Once upon a time a cortège? Well, who knows?

For eighteen years I had studied life after death. In this new opening, there is also a closing, which this book is about. I was always challenged, but never looked back—to the belief existing before the first year of being assaulted by the impression of having the honor to follow a friend, Milton Klonsky, through passageways beyond death.

Now for the first time I am compelled to drop everything introduced earlier, announce the amount of it that was absorbed. And let go. With that consciousness—whatever much of it was retained and mastered—look at the days ahead.

This is necessary, because the debates about *theoretical outcomes of these issues and questions* are idle, so long as we are not in an airtight room.

Being in life, the very *focus on these issues*—or from the other angle, the very fact that the issues were active in our lives or minds—brought their impact to the surface. *Propelled them into an unconscious dynamics*; i.e., unconscious to us because we hadn't the time, what with all we were concerned with, to figure it out.

It is no longer about words. There is a threshold now, where over the horizon, the continuations of these questions *are leading off* from HOW THEY AFFECT US—not as issues up for discussion at a table but in action. *They are moving on*.

This was impressed on me. We will have to know how to defend ourselves against the *implications* of the answers EVEN BEFORE

GETTING TO THE ANSWERS. Because our very *focus had* EFFECT. Also, to help integrate, in view of the expansion of consciousness this inevitably invokes. Invoking the adaptations, we have marched across the century line—all the lines it connects to.

I, for one, had to drop any unfinished questions, urgently needed ON THE FIELD OF ACTION. No longer was it about closed rooms; rather, places where *pieces* of these questions were integrated were encountering each other. AND MORE THAN THAT. Ideologies encountered. Could our minds even HOLD IT? At least, this is how the Earth looked, from a (you might say) Einsteinian angle.

※

We report from a bridge
the left-out important connections in this story
A-BRIDGED.
Jung tells us that Hammurabi was identified with the Age of Aires (the Ram) that led to the Age of Pisces. Milton Klonsky sent me a post card from Greece
It pictured Ulysses escaping the cyclops, the giant Polyphemus, after shoving a hot pole into his eye,
–riding out of the cave he'd been trapped in
strapped to the belly of a ram
Milton commented—
So you put out the outer eye.
What do you do about the
Inner eye?"
The cyclops had only one eye

Johann Sebastian *played his fugues backwards*
AND, to carry this investigation further, Jung said that in his fugues Bach *was in conjunction with the collective unconscious.* Jung did not write further on this matter, to my knowledge, dropping only that clue. A small clue.

Now, in 2002, I held in my hands the cover to the Russian LP album *The Art of the Fugue*, which confirms the information about Bach playing backwards.

Got into the Alpha–Omega

Rhythm

one strand the immediate, the local . . .

Sitting at the piano . . . The piece brought out of storage like a doll on a shelf, we pick up again—no, don't say it—*the seven-year-old me at the piano.*

The "nonlocal" strand of the arpeggio assigned me to play in the recital, in the lapse of my forgetting the ending—the gap of entropy (the sequence of notes, the "order" wiped out, cleared from my brain)—*left the local.* Well, there was still the recourse, the White Knight, in the "nonlocal," though how did the little girl knew this? It must have been in a trance, an ancient instinct, perhaps transpersonal.

No longer influenced only by what was in its surrounding!— inside the dislocation, the momentary jarring absence of memory as to what came next (???)—the other strand *kept going.* What fear had it to sail into or *become* a universal question: *What comes next?*

It generalized (a condition) located as a *continuing situation* that would someday try to answer itself. Not definitively, forever, but in relationship at least to this one lifetime's pattern, even closure, as it lifted itself higher than the local setting—to purpose, possibility, if it hooked in *on a higher frequency*: a continued streamer of a question, something inside the Alpha–Omega, which also asked, What next? And next? And next, how did it fit together and how, then, did it END?

*rbc

Riding out of this time period or at least this lifetime
With a playback—oops, Bach—straight through start to finish
Well, we did it.

Part
Five

Chapter Eight

Electrical Humanity

This is the story of the entry into the electrical era, with blinders on. (Boy, am I really stitching this together—finding sections, a group of pages or just a loose page, stitching them into a unit, but since the message is unified, it's a fit.) To go on without interruption . . .

Yet another link comes in through the idea of particle spies that interact by breaking into closed pairs. Even particles have break-ins. We don't even have to look to genes for this propensity. Look how we've found it down here. So we learned it from the particles Ah-ha. Breaking into particle pairs *and* retrieving the information from one.

Theft of information, we learned there too. It's in the particles in us. Look no further. Then there's "quantum teleportation," transfer of quantum information that leaves one location to arrive at another. Now let's move to particle *spies*: "Operation: Neutrino: How the neutrino went from ghost particle to vital physics tool—a tale of bombs, espionage and subtle flavor," by Professor David Kaiser, July 26, 2017.

Also (by Rahul Rao):

SCIENTISTS FOUND A FLEETING PARTICLE FROM THE UNIVERSE'S FIRST MOMENTS
TO DETECT AN X PARTICLE, MAKE SOME QUARK-GLUON PLASMA

. . .

So there you have it, how you can do it yourself.
In the "magnetic whorl of CERN's Large Hadron Collider (LHC),

the . . . vast majority of that data is fluff that CERN automatically filters out," reports Rao. However, not surprisingly, "hidden gems lie buried deep within these storage banks."

> Particle physicists have uncovered one such gem: a strange particle with a strange name, X(3872). If they're right, it could be a look back into the very earliest flickers of time—what the universe looked like in the first millionth of a second after the Big Bang.[10]

According to Wikipedia:

> The X(3872) is an exotic meson candidate with a mass of 3871.68 MeV/c^2 which does not fit into the quark model . . . . Several theories have been proposed for its nature, such as a mesonic molecule or a diquark-antidiquark pair (tetraquark).
>
> . . . The first evidence of X(3872) production in the quark–gluon plasma has been reported by the CMS experiment at CERN in January 2022.

※

A tetraquark would have four quarks, but the usual subatomic particles—the typical protons and neutrons—are made up of three quarks; "tetraquark particles," Rao explains, "are weird, and usually need high energies to stay together." He elaborates:

> Another possibility is that X(3872) is actually built from mesons . . . Mesons can sometimes appear fleetingly on Earth, when high-energy cosmic rays collide with typical matter. But nobody has ever seen a larger particle made up of multiple mesons.
>
> This is exciting, says [particle physicist Yen-Jie] Lee, because because if X(3872) is created from mesons, then it's a sign that the universe was resplendent with such "exotic" particles.[11]

Jennifer Chu | MIT News Office, January 21, 2022, starts with the familiar: "In the first millionths of a second after the Big Bang, the universe was a roiling, trillion-degree plasma of quarks and gluons—elementary particles that briefly glommed together in

countless combinations before cooling and settling into more sta-
ble configurations . . . to make the neutrons and protons of ordinary
matter." But going on, she brings us up to date:

> In the chaos before cooling, a fraction of these quarks
> and gluons collided randomly to form short-lived "X" parti-
> cles, so named for their mysterious, unknown structures . . .
> Now physicists at MIT's Laboratory for Nuclear Science and
> elsewhere have found evidence of X particles in the quark-
> gluon plasma produced in the Large Hadron Collider (LHC)
> at CERN, the European Organization for Nuclear Research,
> based near Geneva, Switzerland.[12]

But what are these "closed pairs" that "particle spies" are
suspected to break into? Daniel Garisto (in "The Universe Is Not
Locally Real and the Physics Nobel Prize Winners Proved It," in
Scientific American) to the rescue.

In the "simplified and modernized version" of Bell's theorem,
the journal tells us, the entanglement theory of how two particles
in a laboratory experiment come to make a closed pair

> goes something like this: Pairs of particles are sent off in
> different directions from a common source, targeted for
> two observers, Alice and Bob, at opposite ends of the solar
> system. Quantum mechanics dictates that it is impossible
> to know the spin . . . of individual particles, prior to mea-
> surement. Once Alice measures one of her particles, she
> finds its spin to be either "up" or "down" . . . yet when she
> measures up, she instantly knows that Bob's corresponding
> particle—which had a random, indefinite spin—must now
> be down. At first glance, this is not so odd. Maybe the parti-
> cles are like a pair of socks—if Alice gets the right sock, Bob
> must have the left.
>
> But under quantum mechanics, particles are not like
> socks, and only when measured do they settle on a spin of
> up or down. This is EPR's key conundrum.

That is, how can communication over such distances occur if the world is reasonable—if it allows only "local" influences on us (EPR), those you can see, touch, and feel?

Newton once more scratches his head. In all these centuries, has this question not been answered, only made worse? Garisto continues to explain:

> If Alice's particles lack a spin until measurement, then how (as they whiz past Neptune) do they know what Bob's particles will do *as they fly out of the solar system in the other direction?* . . . The odds of correctly predicting this even 200 times in a row are one in 10^{60}—a number greater than all the atoms in the solar system. Yet . . . quantum mechanics says Alice's particles can keep correctly predicting, as though they were telepathically connected to Bob's particles.[13] (my italics)

The article is appropriately titled "The Universe Is Not Locally Real."

> I vividly recall that when I understood the proof of the |above-described Bell| theorem. I went outside in the warm afternoon and sat on the steps of the college library stunned. I pulled out a notebook and immediately wrote a poem to a girl I had a crush on, in which I told her that *each time we touched there were electrons in our hands which from then on would be entangled in each other.* (my italics)
> —Lee Smolin *Einstein's Unfinished Revolution*, Kindle, Preface

※

I recall—when I was twenty-four and smoked my first marijuana cigarette—the incredible vision of the universe sitting on my eyelids, which it appeared to do quite convincingly, I might add, as if X-ray vision.

If so, the Little Dot—

No, no, do not go on. These constructions are not known. Even to myself.

I am about to describe the mystical experience I had once, also at twenty-four, of leaping out of my body to join—nothing more than an instructed, a conscious, Aware dot. An atom? A molecule? A PHOTON? All my vision was interior, enveloped in the sense of the Little Dot, beckoning me from over my head, on steady course.

Now, this dot could not be swayed. I saw that at a glance. It seemed, at that moment, a closed system. Its mission, to it, so clearly powerful.

It was not me but beckoning me. Correct?-

But suppose the Dot *was* me. And why else show herself to me? I listened, completely merged. I was following a dot; and that dot, flying through the universe, evidently on orders that I understood and where they came from.

In this instance, she was pulling me out of the scene in the room I was in. At least, pulling my consciousness out. Why?

Well, I was being eradicated from a situation that—shall we take a guess?—would do me harm to stay consciously in it? Evidently, be apt to produce a physical attraction that blocked out another *dimension* of attraction *on virtually the same coordinates*. Or that could use this as an interception contingency.

To the rescue, the Little Dot. Materializing into view overhead, convincing a startled me, by—was it a signal?—to leave the physical setting.

Instantly I shot out of my body, which I never had, knowingly, before. I *had* to follow.

And now these many—decades—later, I reveal more to myself. For where she "started," I "end." Or rather let us say that she had the capacity to take me past where I was, as in a space capsule, and set me down, in a fait accompli, past the present.

Earlier, I observed: "So this cosmic, primeval pattern of beginning-end expanding into content is like a nugget of Life Form, replicating (giving the shape or image of) the First Origin."

As to size, imagine "not just," said astronomer Owen Gingerich, "this room, or the earth, or the solar system, but the entire universe squeezed into an intense dot of pure energy.

�֍

An image (of a Little Dot beckoning me upward) that could last three, four decades—no, more. I am writing this to calm myself. It did suddenly provide a coordinate. Just like the Mother of the Universe Dot, when it exploded everything we know and can see into existence? Here was the very first pattern in the world.

I must keep going. Find out what the destination is.

And so—on a tangent out of this book I was in, the lifetime on this trajectory—I shot out. I seem to be born? YES OR NO? I don't know yet. At this "point," I don't know a single thing. On the other hand, this Point knows all it needs to. That, I know.

So I held on FOR DEAR LIFE, imagining the only thing I could—that the inexorable focus, more long-sustained than before—this sense that it was focus itself looking through my eyes, and how silly it must look or pretentious (or earnest and-never-as-of-yet-smiling)—that this constant single-pointedness must be the arrival of the best future I could hope for. It was a long-ago choice when during physical loss of what we call virginity—no? yes—through the prism of my mind I escaped and flew from and to I knew not where.

A graded image on a Planck scale? Surely not. But in some dimension where a dot could have consciousness, that part (of me?) showing herself to me—rather abolished me; for though in observing her, I was split from her, I felt it was myself, like looking up, instead of down on the physical self, out-of-body; it was my mind, my concentration, I was both watching and entering, merged with and "locally" separate from; I left the scene in the room and appeared, right on track, in another dimension; though I would not forget this moment of lifting off with her, or it—the details of the trip? Yes, forgotten—entirely.

I get it. I was abolished. My old world was. It needed a fresh start. So the universe sent me its own pattern for Beginnings. How it created itself, or whatever Creator did—it started small, miniscule. Barely noticeable except that it was the only thing around and carried terrific explosive force. And for some reason the bed I was lying in, in the proverbial and physical sense, had to be intercepted. The Little Dot, compressing the intentness of the universe, my universe, when it was leaving one—world, was it?—behind, provided me with a map it knew.

Was it some potential that was conscious of something this scene, in that form, triggered—unforgotten, in her scale of time? Or just some non-incarnated particle aspect of me?

Well, many—that is, a lifetime of—years later, we return to settle this "score"—return to the sequel to this moment (yes, that's more like it. No scores at all), this hope she held out that born as I was, being who I am, in the particle sense, I could be intercepted AT THAT MOMENT; as if (perhaps) the physical love, on the Earth, was omitting what she (my essence) would, in parallel and analogy, show "the other side of—by deleting the scene from memory, but not fact), replacing it with one thing only: the voyage of the Little Dot.

So, on some mission she flew to intercept me? Perhaps the entire soul grouping sent her out. Joined her, in fact.

Thus, this me now here—arrived at in the Timeline that DID occur—hanging on a telephone pole, hoping not to be shorted. Protected perhaps back then, from an alternate reality in the future, starting from there, not taken.

And so it was. I was moved forward—to here. Yes, I was safe, responding as I did, to the introduction to me of her, the Little Dot. She whom I will name in that way, for lack of other name and because it pleases me. So she does know how she got here (and where we went, unremembered by me).

Or do you think it was someone else come to steer me? I do not. The impact was too huge. I also saw her the only time I was hypnotized. No, she was "me," but much "higher," more "minute." Years later, I have wound up here, and that was, evidently, essential to the trajectory she set me on. Secured, at last, that I didn't miss out on by wandering into an entirely

Earth temptation.

I see now why I sensed lately—back here in the literal present—I had been delivered a huge sum of money, perhaps gold bars—or was it silver, or just a treasure of some sort? To be there at the SUMMING UP. In some constellation, cold transcendent (I borrow the concept and some of the words; they could not ever be better put. We will come back to them).*

> Standing, in all this, I think perhaps I can do it—be synchronous with myself,** teach others this possibility; how when there is no help in the environment, they can draw from the self who does not yet exist but is waiting nonetheless, very close by, seeing things entirely differently.
> —*Tricks High Up*

No solution existed at the moment—one's head in one reality, one's hands with a different action command, a different necessity, relative to something entirely different.

So I sit here, entirely inscrutable even to myself. I see myself, feel my features, form my expression. And it is no expression at all. It is myself poured into my eyes—which are looking somewhere I think they can see into. As I said, I don't know. I do know that HOLD THIS FOCUS, I MUST.

---

* Dream September 10: fractions of ground that would deliver oil wells belonged to my father; he should not turn them over; i.e., that I should expect—be on the lookout for—GEYSER SPURTS. Deeply buried information when the digging touched that level. I was instructed to find *which fractions*—not the whole thing—of these underground wells, or buried information, were *meant* to be brought out. Which were part of the natural result of this ground-laying and digging.

** Tricky indeed, said David Bohm, because of the asynchronous (*Wholeness and the Implicate Order*, pages 153–154):

"In this movement [i.e., the explication of a 'whole picture,' or of a slightly different picture, due to how many times we turn the stirring device to bring some dye into explicate form], the 'picture' present at any given moment would consist only of aspects that can be explicated together . . . As events happening at the same time are said to be *synchronous*, so aspects that can be explicated together can be called *synordinate*, while those that cannot be explicated together may then be called *asynodinate*." If synchronous events came together synordinately, it could be the result was synchronicity. This, he did not say. But it FOLLOWS.

To have the universe on one's eyelids must be a new tool—of "shaping" space. Could one consciously "bend" space—how? And not just into one SHAPE.

I remember the guru at the beginning of this book, looking at a photo of his devotees. "He paused over the different eyes, ears, noses, mouths—expressions—transporting energy into them. I saw it. The picture of that moment never left me. I can do that. So . . . he's shown me a secret.* Other people witnessed it. But I don't think they 'saw' it."

Like the guru, who transmitted light and healing to his devotees by looking at a group photo, could one transmit to the universe if it rested on one's eyelids? But I thought nothing like that then. It's a passing thought now. Still, did I get an inkling of a secret?*

A passing thought, nonsense. I feel a rising excitement. This is a secret, isn't it?

---

* I will just call this My birth. The wavelength, of what? Or will I? An *I* that wants to do this steps forth. So it lets us squabble. Still in the dark.

The Flea
O.K. Let's jump into it.

I have brought this up. Indeed, I needed to because no one remembers it now. No matter how great a sensation this essay made at the time, back in the 1960s, when it came out and I read it. Dazzled. That's not exaggerated. We will have to remember or re-imagine the room.

To do that, I am stepping into "a character role." Don't be concerned. It wasn't really me. I *did not write this essay*. But that's beside the point. My imagination can do this. Re-create the situation as if I were the author.

Remember back then. How Klonsky walked around quoting, "For black blooms and it is purple." Yes, don't forget Christopher Smart, choosing the cast, having them come, the help we need. Out of memory, striding forth, as we hold the focus so that they can COME IN THROUGH IT. Who said there was nothing in "ether"? They walk in, in the very ether or the memories, in the surrounding enhancement this kind of matter adds. That is, the immaterial matter in the setting of the mind.

So I turn my mind over to this, as the focus holds.

Yes, it IS HELD. Like looking to see if some glue has stuck (gluons, no doubt)—was it strong enough? We go back to that day in 1973. Emerge from the room; he had been in a sort of consciousness underground (perhaps our very own), where certain things were obvious if one could find the ways they connected. Not winding at all if one knew how[*]

And so he made the discovery, which went for the most part unprobed further. Well, not understood, though many, like me, dazzled, sensed he was onto something, narrating—with a physical-reality description, so as to be comprehensible—the patchwork

---

[*] Chaos barely had a name then. There was scarcely a "butterfly" question—though the initial presentation on it, "The Essence of Chaos," by Edward Lorenz, had taken place among academics in 1972, then been published for the layperson in 1993. So no one noticed—what with the central formulation of "chaos" restricted to the American Association for the Advancement of Science and this one still in my head, in NYC–that THERE MIGHT BE A CONNECTION.

quilt in which connections ran below the surface of our reality: revealing it to us in the unlikely spots in which, in history, what cropped up? The flea. But that was just for starters.

For instance, how the flea drove Newton into the countryside to discover that everything acted on everything else. That is, it means (I guess) there is nothing born without a sense of something. And that something, be it only a sense of its environment (the composition of dust in the air around it or whatever), gives it that thing we call "gravity"—that attraction. In that it "knows" what it needs to know? And is drawn to where that knowledge has completion or application? And that knowledge exists in "tracks," places traveled down before, created as indentations by mere "existence," "presence," itself? And all together, unseen and certainly unheeded by us, because we don't know where to look, these group messages sprout up? Who would think to connect the appearance of the flea down into everyday reality, causing the Plague, was more than an irrelevant coincidence, not part of a Grand Weaving in a Tapestry of Connections?

Every created thing has that thing (some called it instinct) that works toward its survival; else the non-equalization of the fact that something drew it to be born and that it equally by law, then, was not tricked (as Descartes felt he established—that God, that is, was not tricking *him*—neither, we say, could he, or she, be tricking a plant or any creature at all). So this insures some kind of attraction, also some sense of "gravity" attraction, toward its survival. But we have jumped way afield.

We have gotten the first clue to what that might be, through the Klonsky essay: "Art & Life: A Menippean Paean to the Flea; or, Did Dostoevsky Kill Trotsky?" I stumbled onto the full significance, observing the face of the writer as he "emerged" from working on it; and, further, I had a second instruction in it in my initiation in Zurich. Yes, the connection is now clear—through words like "informatics" and "chaos theory"; one can from there coherently speak. It can now be seen that the implications in this essay—on the Earth—are a piece of the missing picture. Even link.

To go back to the field now, the very field, where he

MADE THE CATCH of this far-flung "ball." But in something like a practice session. Perhaps this too is a practice session. We are there now, in—ah-ha—OUT field. Yes, OUTfield. We know our one job. And so we must say, fearful or not (we are not fearful), that—erase even the notion—this focus says this principle of gravity, of things attracted through mass making indentations, curves, punch marks that went in and that the next arriver followed, roads round mountains that meant all the cars went in circles— Well, this principle only revealed a theory of PATTERN. Pattern, however, *like the range of vision, as it related to light and even to perception, like the spectrum of visible light*, had many ranges itself. And some of these ranges of patterns were invisible—

Yes, I know, you know about "psychological patterns." But you do not know that they are "physical" too, to the parts and processes of us, such as are down in the particle world. They establish "tendencies."*

---

* Newton rubbed his chin. Ah. Let's begin.

To explain such things as an archangel (Gabriel talking to Mohammed) or a reincarnational memory, physicist Amit Goswami draws on a term he thinks will do: "This [a birthmark] suggests [he speculates and then answers himself] that a memory of the vital body was transmitted via the quantum monad from one incarnation to the next. . . .

"I agree," he says. "The subtle body in the form of the quantum monad is the carrier of the attributes of one's life to the next" (page 144).

Was the Little Dot a "quantum monad," appearing at a critical moment, making it an "entry point"; or even was she flying out of a scene corresponding to that one, on the physical level, but AS SHE KNEW IT much higher up? To where? and in what time scheme? Taking me, like Scrooge, somewhere to view my life IF I stayed conscious in the scene and did not leave it, with her? My body? No matter if that continued on in the scene. "I" had been whisked away and "educated." Like, I was saying, Scrooge. Was that it?

Taking me—? We have answered, speculatively, TO HERE. We will stop everything else and wait for her, staring up at the sky, checking the body temperatures, saying we are ready, I am ready, Let the play begin. Let her enter THIS VERY SECOND if she will. Curtains up, please. Yes, like the Buddha under the fig tree

waiting for his lost consciousness to arrive.

And come it did.

But a hindsight connection also comes to the fore: if it was Jibril (Gabriel) who told Mohammed to read/recite (I only realized this now), then is there some deep-into-the-Universe "connection" with the day I saw a parade that coincided with the death of Milton Klonsky, unknown consciously to me—the Universe in that way sending me a signal? The instant afterwards, when I asked my then-husband what the parade was for, he answered (chidingly, amusedly, as a spoof? OR IN DIVINE INSPIRATION, giving a platform of setting)—he answered, "The day that Mohammed was told to write." How incongruous.

Yet—on the theory I am proffering and pursuing—were "they"—the paraders, in another dimension, welcoming Milton as if from a victory, showing me that connection between the two moments, in deeper terms (no matter what induced him to give that answer). I was totally brought up abrupt when Jan made this offhand remark.

Offhand? Well, apparently so. But was it? *The command to write came from*

Gabriel, said Mohammed Surely, this parade was not in alignment. Surely, Gabriel wasn't again at work.

But he didn't have to be. Alignment would do the trick.

But alignments can run for large-scale events starting an entire religion or small-scale, even miniscule, events. Were, even at that moment, the paraders "announcing" the death in *some Other World double track* (my then-husband being the type to follow inspiration spontaneously) from whatever high-answer level the parade was emerging out of (in the physical-level drama representing the intangible aftermath of death. The parade striking me dumb, mute, in its uncalled-for—seemingly—powerful numinosity, though, right then and there locally appearing to me to be heralding some unknown triumph? Later, I interpreted it to be triumph (but how?) of Milton's life plan. Which, unavoidably, as a signal, harks back to the 1965 signal to "begin" I got from watching a beggar in Paris. "Begin!" Yes, I did. Harking to the "private" signal both times. A little more on that ahead, in the new information it brings.

Stowed away in the large, known symbolic events—that is, events that became symbols to us, in this case, Mohammed being told to write, were connections that I could ride the coattails of, or stow away in the transportation of, so the signal said.

Lift it to the correlation with Gabriel speaking instructions to the illiterate Mohammed—what is *the connecting "pattern"*: presuming you can get to a level of interpretation and understanding by finding out what "gravity" forged "the connection," i.e., the repeated track; i.e., the returning "memory"????

Or something else.

A very obtuse way of asking if gravity (or a familiar track) had anything to do with it, THEN what was it???? Gravity dangling a pattern and saying: *Over here. Step into this one.* Numinosity leading the way.

Again, as with the Little Dot, holding up a sign on the invisible life path.

This happens all the time, by the way—with invisible warnings, clues, pssts so loud subtly that you can almost hear them.

We do not dare to bring up, but we'd better, that it could also have been a moment when TWO different instances were being cross-fertilized for the Earth, albeit unknown to it; for instance, the birth of the Christ, when Gabriel announced it in advance; then the command of Gabriel to Mohammed—which led to two terrestrial religions. And then now to have *this* connection with Gabriel in celebration, AT THE MOMENT ANNOUNC-ING A DEATH, a death I am to speak on for decades: what was BEING COR-RELATED into the strings and fortunes, or slings and arrows, of the Earth surrounding "fields"? What was GOING ON, or ARRIVING, if we want to see it that way? And I for one surely had better take that slant.

Yes, slant, exactly so. Was this then the slant I followed my mother down, in birth, in which an entering larger presence also arrived—was that happening here? Thus, the to-be OMEGA, or larger understanding, with light for the next century, who had signaled me across a window—Amit Goswami calls it, "the Visionary Window." A *larger presence that could sum up, point the way through the twentieth century issues? Or be prepared to conclude every-thing after the new Alpha of the time period had done its work?*

This yet another critical "window," again bringing the charge to Write! And how often did it whisper in an ear? (I finally get wind of the connec-tion here too)—reaching diametrically directly to Paris, that window at the Dôme Café—*and who knows how many other points not connected with me?* But as I was saying, the command to "write!" accosted me yet again, in a plane in the 1990s, as I looked out the window. What did I see but sparks of fire—that's right, saying "Fire on the broadside!"? —came not in the form of a cigarette being lit, but of a "wing" on fire. That incident, too, heavily laden with the injunction to W*rite!*

All of it part of this ball of "yarn"—yes, yarn—that Penelope is unroll-ing, saying the same thing. And that leads right to my question about how it was wrapped up in these images. Kinetic. Nonverbal. But clear as day!

Part
Six

Chapter Nine

The setting: Somewhere between Coney Island and heaven
The occasion
Angels in chorus
Mighty fortress
Word of God become flesh
Scribes of before, tell us how the Earth's future is being intercepted
Tell us who is leading us to this door
and THROUGH this door (bell) short of this we will be no more
Come, scribes of the past

henceforth to be called our Daemon
like the Socratic daemon
now congregated in one body
to usher in
the future of the Earth

two warriors locked in battle
each calling itself a doorway to the future of the Earth
and the Earth itself not let in one the secret
not let in on the reality of the atmosphere it is in
calling it Earthquakes and commonsense
everyday names
and every which you will
calling it everything but the real
come to us, now if you will: The Real

And so with rolled-up diplomas in hand and white-gowned in a
band

They marched forward, those who had been chosen
with many turned away but these chosen and here to stay
to be the Leaders of the Transition

How there are people within the body of us
The Earth's physical potential
The physical who live on the Earth
taking us, still within us
to our higher potential
and doing this for love of the Earth

Whose love for the Earth?
Who could love her so much?
As she turns in the traumas of
A planet's
Rebirth

For all these reasons they gathered together
Men and women I could not see
So I had to learn to believe in
What I could not see
They said they had come
So time would be no more as before

To open to the Earth the window into eternity
They said they had come to do this
And I must quickly harken and speak
For even as they told me, the moment was passing

They were not prisoners of time, like me
And they even announced a new shift in Time itself
That Time as we knew it was no more to be
They announced a meeting point in space
As in a summit between nations
And at that point no violations

Abruptly, midway through the page, it ends. But enough said. Received.

I must stop to tell you what AI just did. It intruded a photo with mouth moving, a female, and she had cartoon words, as her mouth silently moved, "My feelings won't change. I'll always love you." That such power between the dimensions exists! *And such humor!* And putting the words into the mouth of a cartoon female.

Not AI. Using an AI cartoon. It was handy.

Underscoring a dream from the night before. Saying: I *mean it.*

As I was saying: back to my almost-favorite topic, focus, message to report:

The body can plug into a TV set. NO?! Plug into a TV set. It can channel *in* the electricity, re-creating the images and responses into its own life. Not, of course, unless it has the predisposition to. Not unless, looking out into the universe, unbeknownst to you, to me, it looks for supports, companions, replicas and agree-ers with its intent, even its impulse, its shadow impulse even. Or its very timid, but best self even. And where it can find agreement, a model, a live enactment of its intent, even fantasy? Well, it's right there on the screen. Don't think our inner impulses are unable to connect the dots and see: *Ah-ha. Just as I thought. My wish lived on screen, a bit modified and camouflaged, albeit. But I recognize it. I'll jump into the field, the pool, the outline,* as if with a pattern for a knitted sweater. That simple. Modules are "out there." Rather, right in my living room. And so it "logs" it for, perhaps, the very next day. Still you, I, are not in the loop. No one tells us. Though I admit, having learned this in Zurich, I am usually in the loop. Not that, usually. I can control the still-unconscious, very very subtle signals and the "plans" kept secret from me.

t could be proved that these other caus
them to electricity; looking for connectio
had not known how to measure or fii
nconscious "program" was "received" IF
time. How to measure unconscious-to-u
How detect that something outside hum:
NTUM TIME???? followed by feeling tl
)lacement was occurring. The fact th
.   . .   .   .   .   ᴄ

It could be proved that these other causes did exist, looking
for connections or available for receipt as triggers, as mirrors; we
had not known how to measure or even *find* interactions where an
unconscious "program" was "received" IF it kept interactive under
the surface. Or just received the input. AND—took it from there.
How to measure unconscious-to-us quantum "registering"?

How to detect that something outside human time was NOW
IN QUANTUM TIME??? How to know when a displacement was
occurring/ The fact that it was something of a holodeck situation,
the world of television?

WE, all of us, SET FORTH FROM THIS DAY (UNCONSCIOUSLY) patterns, premonitions, situations that we, or someone, will make events of. For we did it for so long, pushing our unconscious away, our wholeness pattern, that lo and behold one day IT BECAME VISIBLE. That is, it thrusts itself into the TV set and elsewhere, all over the Earth, as things that were NOT DONE. That is, wish fulfillment, acts deemed "immoral." As "when and how" standing at the door, with this jump start, perhaps eve of a "dead generator," had little say.

But the small thing that "escaped" our "observation" was merely this; and it is all I was able to capture that day. It was: these patterns, THEY DO NOT STAND STILL IN ONE PLACE.

"And this shall be a sign unto you."

You shall find the babe
wrapped in"—literature.

How so?

Well, this bring us right back into the neglected but secretly hidden variable, the essay through which we were (I was) introduced, namelessly—before it was widely circulated as a variant idea—to the chaos theory.

It was the upside-down side of itself. Pinned upon the dead body of a Flea. Nothing to look at there.

On the other hand—

Looking beneath the hidden variable of the minuscule insect that carried germs—but shaking it, fleecing, to find out what was in some pocket—taking it to a different order of reality— it was the FLEA that not only carried terrible-disease germs. Using it covertly like this, it could carry an IDEA, buried in the underside of itself. Exactly as unconsciously, it had been the underside of the conditions that caused Newton to go into retreat, and his ideas break through time and descend to us. Yes, the flea did not hinder him. He thought in privacy, unimpeded by it and the germs it (secretly to the inhabitants of that era) carried. For here was the "cause" of the plague, though they knew it not.

All the while, the unknown instigator, or carrier, of the plague that was killing people was all that was to be seen on the surface. One person giving birth to the ideas of the next centuries (as if a compacted, non-digressing point, one could say)—its science foundation. But the idea relevant to that—the procedure—remained unconscious; people had enough to do to discover the carrier, the germs in their properties, much less to go even further AND MAKE A CONNECTION with Newton.

To go from the unknown physical cause of disease, germs (when still further ahead, DNA, as the genetic instrument of heredity was also unknown), to keep on jumping and get to the associative gestalt layout, the geography, the "map" that Newton was looking for, it would take a great flight of the imagination. Like driving down a one-way highway, in the wrong direction, the direction no one else was going in.

Where was the map? he wanted to know.*

---

* Not having scientific laboratories, the earliest scientists checked and measured by what the stars were doing at the time. "You see, for them," reports "Universe Unriddled" (in "Ancient Astronomical Observatories and Their Significance"), "the sky was like a giant storybook, filled with tales of gods, heroes, and mythical creatures. But it was also a practical tool, helping them navigate, keep time, and even survive." But looking back in history for the Plan, Newton could not find it.

Could not—with his comprehensive mind—find final causes, could not find anything at all that verified the assumption of a Maker, who had a Plan. The Plan must be a hidden variable. He did not see (not knowing about germs) that the very predicament—or situation—he was in was also itself the map of the gestalt *In an invisible synchronicity, or polar (or multidimensional, illustrated) energetics, the masses were dying, and Newton was discovering how mass is related to gravity* ("In Newton's theory every least particle of matter attracts every other particle gravitationally," Britannica Encyclopedia), *and gravity is in some ways indifferent to mass* ("he showed that the attraction of a finite body with spherical symmetry is the same as that of the whole mass at the centre of the body," Britannica); *or how gravity is a force that holds things in place and affects speed of motion.*

But this clue of the relationship of mass to gravity had further distances to go—albeit that slews of literal, physical masses (with souls and spirits, mind you) were slain to the ground, in the invisible illustration at the other pole. The *mass mind was dying*, at the side of Newton, as this information that would lead to a theory of mass began slowly to set the foundation for its entry eventually *into* the mass mind itself, charging in.

Now, on the one hand, Newton thought light was ONLY points, not waves. So this inhibited him from seeing the poles of the idea as THE SAME IDEA, in two forms, one aspect of it being compacted, as it were, in him, and *the disperse reflection* in the people, all through the population, inhabiting (in many cases) corpses.

For his pole of light, as it were, there was (on the other end of the spectrum, dying out) the old: the deprived-of-light (of Life Force), the now-darkness. While he remained upright. OR most of the time in fact in bed, THINKING, formulating the theory of force that in fact was acting itself out right in the then-current situation, which was representative (just as any envoy) OF THE IDEA.

But this theory acting itself out also was carrying the matter so far as to illustrate LIFE force. Synchronicity, or unconscious archetypical activity, that no one—mind you, it would have been impossible—saw, even in the most flickering glimmer. This clue would keep right on moving, even to Einstein, where it would knock the daylights out of him, as he himself said—in shock. But not kill him, physically. On that point, he stood with Newton, alive, made so by the force of the idea that set to light in him, calling him father and thus giving him the strength to survive, many a long later year.

This is all I know at this time.

Now, what I picked up that day, standing in the doorway, preparing for today, knowing one day I would throw everything up but this one thought, was that these patterns, these sequences, like the very DNA chains, even the seemingly throwaway ones— That they hold on to their shape. JUST LIKE YOU AND ME.*

---

* I have discovered—to my amazement—that the reason I did not use names of characters, but rather jumped ahead, using my own name (my "I") in all the optional places, was that—relief, at last—I saw that the future would understand it; that is, when we began to look for ourselves in overlappings and other ways, IN SO MANY PLACES. Not just standing there as a viewable, physically defined AND LOCATED, linearity-bound single individual, born and with a brand name tacked forever onto us. So I anticipated. This is one of the greatest reliefs of my life—to find out that I am just as much a fiction writer as anyone.

Only, by view of the fact that I am not studying my mathematical self, in the precise sense of preexisting mathematical formulas for me, I am studying my artistic self, the one who will exist at the end of the creation and with all the displaced, left-behind personalities either close to or far from the end product's sense of self. By the clear law I am about to discover, this will make total sense: that I have the right to declare the expedition I am on FROM THE START. Rather than to in surprise declare it at the end. When it is too late to assume the responsibility I did BY DOING IT OPENLY, calling it by name, saying it had the role of "I" all along, when of course in many ways it clearly didn't. The times in which I was camouflaged, unconscious, being outpassed, passed by, cast off. Speculating and not commitedly in the description. Murdered, as rightly I should have been, the times when I hadn't A CLUE WHO I WAS OR WHAT I WAS DOING.

So I kept the trail in full view, calling the invented characters (I was living through) myself, or an "I" experiencer, rather then Molly, Julius, Raskolnikov, etc. This would have been another option. I greatly regretted that I did not seem to push the energy away. Rather, I drew it up close. But up close, however imaginary, it suddenly told me IT WAS "I." I could not resist. I knew not why. I had no conscious knowledge then OF THE LAW ON IT. Why could not I be a fiction writer? Why did the characters

———————————————

TELL ME DIFFERENT. Seek me out, from within my own life? Why did they not STAY ON BOOK PAGES. But they began increasingly, at a rather early BUT WHERE? Where would you look if this one, the you in your body, was not enough so for you to feel convinced it WAS THE REAL THING? WHERE WOULD YOU LOOK?

So these laws of energetics became real to me. I remembered the visitor—the me that shot down through all the atoms and electricities at seven—who *walked right in, thinking inside my head*, astonished to see the plight I (the one in form as a child) was in.

For he, seemingly in the same state of astonishment as I, was a known writer, self-aware, who expected to have been much further along by the age of seven (or who remembered having been, *whether from the future or the past* or even a different planet or universe, for all I know), and whose astonished queries (to herself/himself, to anyone), I listened in on.

Or, in fact, THOUGHT. Yes, these were my thoughts, suddenly, when this energy began to do soul-searching. But this I had a different history, obviously, one could confidently deduce, based on the assertions it made (to itself) in my head.

And let me tell you, there was no doubt whatsoever, then, that THAT WAS the real one. But how to walk out of this one, TO THAT ONE? Anyway, there was THEN such a huge age difference. No more than in a marriage, could a huge age gap between oneself and oneself be sustained. Now? NOW, well, I had better hurry if to find that one in this lifetime at all. And even that, I realized, was fatal now. No, right now, I had to just—standing here in this present body—DECLARE that the real I was me. AND HERE I WAS; i.e., project the energy I was sure was me.

And hadn't I clearly seen it? Didn't I know what it felt like, the day it came—as another me—inside the familiar me, the seven-year-old child? I knew how it felt if you weren't expecting it. I knew how it had felt to me. I knew how to feel it NOT "at a distance." So there must be some *action at a distance* that made it a law that there was a way to be your real self.

age, to find me FIRST inside the life pages. Then how could I imagine them when they had already imagined themselves INSIDE MY LIFE.

Taking me not by imaginary storm, but life storm. Storming into my life, calling themselves—outrageously and inexplicably—I. *How dare they?*

I never said this. Patiently, I said yes every time. I, like you, had no defense. I did not know about the energetics of I. I weep now, thinking of some of the I *I* lost. Some of the I portions I took like pieces of pizza. No, I knew not how to say energetically "yes, I truly want you here. But you, how did you even ever think YOU MIGHT BE ME." No, I never ever knew the way it worked. So I now tell you the law I discovered. For you to know at birth, at five years old. Later. But not so late as I.

And it still leaves you all the laws left in the universe—plenty—to discover by yourself. Fortunately for me, the real I did once pay a visit at seven years old. And also knew the theories of all this. Planned through the thicket, like the one in wallpaper panels in my childhood room, to find me and convince me THIS was the real I. If I, in the remnants of my energetics, still had enough of me to join the bandwagon and go where this I was going. Catching me off-guard, telling me it was a day to judge, in earnest. And could I? Could I recognize myself, after all the imposters had done their "dirty work." As happens here on Earth, when we look at our clown and sad-sack clothes and take them for our energetic options. No, this was the end of the Old Earth. I wanted to offer this Law up to it. Like a mighty kite that sailed through infinity, proclaiming a truth that I (the real one) was long committed to. I had allowed much transgression and trespassing. What would it feel like if, with no law to explain it to you, the REAL REALITY of your energetics presented itself one day?

And if you recognized that, you would understand the whole law by which it waited so late to do so. AND YOU DIDN'T SUSPECT A THING. At least, not enough so to just walk out and look for yourself somewhere else. To *be* that self. But this was the second law I was discovering. Even as a second law of thermodynamics. That you must at least BE that self *before it degenerated and wasted away in expiring energy*. No, there was a thermodynamic law for the SELF energy ALSO. The fact was, though, that the self who arrived (or woke up) in me, when I was age seven, for a definitively real second of infinity, as it were, in full cognizance of who he/she was, HAD NO MEMORY OR AWARENESS OF ME. But imagined or assumed that a tangent between himself (I detected him to be a "he") would never be found in a childhood such as I was having: SO ASLEEP, so mute—I sputter to try to say more. It was as if some child such as Mozart, or a known writer, looking around with amnesia about the childhood, arrived, somehow, inside one's (my) child frame and wondered what was going on, because nothing made sense anymore—putting the outside references BESIDE THE INNER!! Perhaps it was here I was first surreptitiously introduced to the concept of "measure me," which I later put into poetry Perhaps it was even implying a relationship with relative time already achieved in some consciousness that propelled him into me—OR ON SOME PLANET?? These laws, then, I am about to discover. Right here. Right now.

0W

Now, this is important, if we are to learn all we can, using just our few facts—or rather, taking them as far as they can be taken. Let's go on.

We must also remember (or rather, hurry)—in that after electronic chips (in the new technology), the presiding energy might be light; and then, folks, fueling the data processing, the very computers that we sit in front of, will possibly be—none other than: DNA.

And so, not to frighten anyone, but to bear down to brass tacks, the truth in fact is that we are surrounded by OUR OWN TRACKS. It matters not that we displaced them (we "observed" only, we made "virtual," we "read" only), from the energy point of view; WE RE-ENFORCED. We made "more likely." We worked in "odds and predictions." About us. Our world. Our children. Our conscious/unconscious divisions of labor. Ha. Stop. Am running out of steam. Of X-rays to look at here.

ILL

These patterns, parallel to and rigorously obeying the laws of our DNA chains, were in fact event chains, the way *they "saw."* One wasn't to think events just combined themselves out of nothing. But of course one didn't think that. Instead, one thought patterns were an accident. But the world—ah, the world. It had MEMORY.

Little Book—*Notes or cut fragments*

I quote from Klonsky's "Flea" essay with a little help from the computer by way of arrangement:

Newton had spent years invested in an alchemical search for the Great Plot in history. The established Newton's ideas were generally accepted in science. Klonsky had much to say about the little-emphacized Newton's search for THE GREAT PLOT.

The article is unknown enough and remarkable enough to quote at length:

Newton had conceived the Principia," he declared in the Preface, 'with an eye upon such principles as might work with considering men for the belief of a diety.' But what worked out instead was the reverse, for it became more and more plain to 'considering men,' even in his own time, that a hypothetical diety did not have to be feigned in order to uphold his system: the Cosmic Machine, being self-adjusting, could run along forever without Him; and besides, as Newton himself acknowledged, such 'a god, without dominion, providence, and final causes, was nothing else but Fate and Nature.' So who needed Him? . . . Set adrift, as 'twere, in this abandoned universe, without a terminus a quo or terminus ad quem, Everyman was thus left to chart a course through absolute space and time by dead ratiocination alone.

*b0W

Didn't Jung and Wolfgang Pauli assert there was a world of psychic reality—a world of archetypes—that mediated between matter and mind?

So, one day a scarab as the mediator knocked at Jung's door (pardon, window) to illustrate—? "Synchronicity. From out of the Egyptian information system, it came.

But no one picked up that facet of what it meant. Sent as instigator of the role the scarab represented, a reminder of what the world of nature taught through each of its "instruments."

And let me tell you, humans, back then, paid attention. Attention was like dues, insurance of survival. So they learned from each other. Man learned very carefully, and it could be that this capturing by observation and empathy, imbibing, imagining, even sometimes using magical thinking, allowed humans to add to their DNA, in some mysterious sympathy, these animal attributes, such as we are focusing on here, the instance of what the scarab taught the pharaoh.

And then it turned round and became the instrument of knowledge for Jung, which after all, is what it had been for the pharaoh, the illustration of a survival technique, a clever point of intelligence, a strategy before a mightier power. See what the lowly scarab does in confrontation with the rising Nile? So they all sat around and they listened back then, and they put it into

OUR GENES.

I see that Faulkner is back. Yes, he says, picking up the thread. What the Egyptians did with the scarab—in learning timing—got passed down in a quite different style to old Jung. At his window. But he did not think of Egypt and Nile banks and how they would overflow and get a tiny creature if he wasn't incredibly smart. What did Jung think of? HE THOUGHT OF TIME. Something more abstract, but certainly as mighty as the Nile. Yet that further connection was never made.

Then I saw it active again one day, being buried, the beetle, in a tomb, that could have stepped right out of Egypt—though it was a sand tomb on a beach—and I paid attention too, just like Old Jung. ONLY, I HADN'T A CLUE WHAT IT MEANT. It could have been like Thomas Mann's character, in "Death in Venice," observing. So I observed. I watched that beetle being buried, already dead, in a large sand tomb. I watched the long walkway of twigs being laid out, Back to where?

The butterfly became the symbol of chaos theory, as a demonstration of it was drawn from the wing flap. In fact, the beetle and the butterfly, in the psyche, have a common history.

The two symbols, sharing a communication bond—were they, scattered and fragmented, a piece of the same message, the same idea, coming in FOR OUR TIMES!!

The same consciousness, arriving by diverse roots, the same smashing of the vessel of *how the Earth used to think*? That is, in separate pieces of the deeper links, which were also viable bits of history, not taken to the general, broad themes that modern times could make of them if it took the idea from the beetle and the butterfly—synergized and KINETIC. As if the stored energy of the accepted symbol in Egypt built up over time, enough energy to turn kinetic for us. Out of the apparent emptiness, where diving and darting photons and muons and what-not played.

So from the light square side of the equation, NOT STATIC, the Earth thought was beginning TO MOVE. The static pieces one by one.

This century answered some of the questions, not addressing others—in fact, answered a lot of questions we never asked; thus, did not wonder about. So let us ask some more And, by the way, once it was broken, if we repaired a thing mechanically, the tracks—what happened to them?—were they erased too?

I had been given the clue of the flea—a kind of gravity swerve of the psyche. That the psyche, just like the cars on the highway, follows "ROUTES." And then I had the Little Dot, the capacity to "PUT IT ALL TOGETHER."

The scarab disappears till it is safe to reappear. Thus, its eggs survive. Like putting up a sign saying: ANYBODY LOOKING FOR ME, I'M OUT TO LUNCH.

For a few months, albeit. Thus, on the narrow scale of the natural, illustrating a universal process of holistic sharing of time and space—to survive. And the pharaoh knew this. He designated the scarab to represent (though the word to us is "immortality") the word, to him, of "timing."

Now they didn't verbalize the explanation so that we understood it in the hieroglyphs, where you might see a row: the sun, a Third Eye, the snake, and the scarab. Representing the powers of the pharaoh.

Well, to belong in such a list, the scarab had to have some pretty strong characteristics, so that it was not the bull or the bird or the camel that stood in this list, but the tiny outsmarter of the raging overflow of the Nile. It spoke to the dramatic side of the brain. It demonstrated a law of nature. The Egyptians did not say this in a way that we picked it up. They just posted it. And we called it something else.

Called "dung beetles," the *Scarabaeus sacer* insects have the practice of shaping animal dung into balls and rolling them to their nests. Once there, the insects lay their eggs inside the dung ball, giving them protection, warmth, and a food source for the soon-to-be-hatched eggs. This behavior puzzled the ancient Egyptians, who thought the scarab eggs were "spontaneously generated" from the dung balls.

Unsurprisingly, these peculiar dung beetles quickly made their way into Egyptian myths. The ancient people in the region came to believe that the sun "ball" was also rolled in the sky in a similar manner, and therefore |portrayed| the god Khepri as a scarab-headed deity. Khepri was the god tasked with the job of helping the sun to rise every morning, i.e., to roll it across the sky.[14]

Then, wrapped in all this lore, it came right to Carl Jung's window and knocked. And here part of the meaning got dropped by the wayside.

So we will leave it there a bit, to return once this idea has fully sunk in!!!

What has just become conclusive here, and what we are trying to establish, is timing, which, appearing in Ancient Egypt, became an established law (or association); the scarab came down to us, meaning here (to the Egyptians) cyclic resurrection. Of course, there were several variations, then and there.

But our scarab, the one that tunnels underground, meant timing.

Now it reappeared, just like Aristotle and other lost parts of our history, in the West, one day when Jung was staring out a window and chanced to see it coincidentally just after a patient told him she'd dreamed, the night before, of a scarab beetle. Time melted. (Can time do that? Or can the human brain in some way melt, into the river of time?)

Chance itself that day, taking a mighty leap forward, liaisoned more emphatically than ever, at least in the West formally, with the concept of "timing." But this was what it was known for back then, in Egypt? How is this possible? It is NOT POSSIBLE.

Unless some mechanism that it demonstrated to the Egyptians was, in some symbol realm, or information technique or realm, being REdemonstrated. To us. Only, did we get it? Well, Jung did. He got part of it. But no one put the scarab under the microscope, like the flea, which was, by the way (under the laws we are now uncovering), teaching us some mighty important and spectacular principles, to put into this discussion.

Q

We now recognize spacetime as a quantum "location" system in which mass pulls to it (warps) all other mass. Yet, mysteriously, "most of the gravity in the universe comes from an invisible source called 'dark matter'" (NASA, "How Gravity Warps Light"). So as gravity is busy warping space, at the same time, it's warping time? How astonishing. Time not only accommodates different viewers and is different at different speeds. Here, we learn that "dark matter" is jumping into the mix in 4-D.

Obviously, the scarab represented—survival. A kind of materialization/dematerialization principle, dependent on moving things around—in that case physically, but not only—due to the conjunction of the *right space and time*. And *disappearance, in between*. Ah, this instinctive knowing, that observing it, the ancient Egyptians incorporated into a symbol. Yes? No?

But Elsasser points out, provocatively and convincingly, that all storage mechanisms of living things have these two forms: the mechanical and this other thing—the one the beetle represented to the pharaonic mind. The one it wanted to be like. To take over the powers of. So that it *represented* some of those powers, like the association with the sun. Or the cobra, the Kundalini (often pictured coming out of the Third Eye of the pharaoh, those millennia into the past). So out of Egypt (which means other ancient cultures as well), we are picking this up. This to put into our collection of what our heritage, our collective mind, Learned.

C

Now, what we retained of it is something else.

⬟

One more warning to the reader. (Or perhaps only to myself.) In addition to its habitual signatures, each one of which it added on a separate page, the computer is inserting yet another section of blank pages, establishing timing of text.

Supposing I manage to conquer the first section of blank pages, get to the top of that mountain, looking out over vistas of the pages already written and that I now connected to this section—but a short distance further, beyond the connecting island, I will run into a second blank section, of living pages that add to themselves, in heterogeneous reproduction, more blank pages. What to do?

A further problem is that this file has now multiplied to 800 pages. But no matter. PROCEED. What have we turned up with our shovel: the connection between two appearances of the scarab beetle IN TIME. It disappeared into total non-comment except in the dusty history books and symbol explications for further centuries. Remaining a bit in decorative fashion.

But to us in the West, it did not soundly make its presence known till the modern twentieth, where Jung quickly realized, in a snap comprehension, that it was illustrating synchronicity.

"Timing" had returned, in the nick of time—demonstrating how *it knew exactly when and where to be someplace, just as if it had an appointment there.* OR *as if time could move things around, on a board.* Which is what synchronicity, by definition, apparently does.

Jung dropped the matter, like a hot coal, into the un-understanding consciousness of the Earth. It could never figure it out—exactly what was this thing?

Similarly (?), synchronistically, one day in Paris, as I sat at the Dôme Café in Montparnasse, a beggar signaled at a window. To me. Now, he wasn't a scarab. WAS THAT IMPORTANT???

Neither was he Cathy, signaling through a window one stormy night in *Wuthering Heights*, that she was alive as a ghost. Very unmistakably, he was a beggar. The sign he gave, elaborate in its kinesthetic demonstration—it looked like *a wave, this looping, curvy, up-down movement of his mouth.* Ah-ha.

It *was* a wave, part of it?

Perhaps made by some mouth that had the capacity to communicate THAT SURVIVED.

Or did it take the place of a wall, and this was the biblical "writing on the wall"? Then we would have pivoted ourselves back to the Book of Daniel.

So this window, "tapped on"—was back in action. But here, wait a minute, now, to the insiders back in Ancient Egypt, this symbol in fact meant that time was a thing one knew how to step into AND STEP OUT OF.

And further, the scarab was like not only x^2 of itself, but x^4, by doubling or exponentially identifying with its meaning, in *two* different cultures, disappeared this time, not into Nile mud with its eggs (underground), but the very *underground of our collective mind.* The very sewers of its junctures avoided, by *not being there.* Nowhere to be found, discussed, contaminated. No siree, not the scarab. Not till it was ready.

The very references obliterated till it could come back up, reappear with no associations except those it brought. So, we are asking:

> to understand synchronicity, is it necessary to understand the scarab beetle? No, it could have come to us another way. But it happened *this way.* In this pursuit of the themes of the new century, very strangely, we are using an insect—once again—to *demonstrate new ideas. Or the routes consciousness uses.* Those ideas that slip through, uncontaminated. Suddenly *there.* How, of course, the signal arrived undistorted by error is another question.

Part Seven

Chapter Ten

Awareness as a Storage Mechanism

True awareness can be a frozen moment—so Faulkner had intuited.

Not using the word, but now he knew that's what it was. His own awareness told it to him—being a master of the stunning, grotesque, gothic, extreme moment; the moment when awareness struck forever, and never moved (becoming a dynamic force, even a daemon, though in the sense of causing focus, movement, motive. But not, in these cases, the kind of daemon he had; free of psychology, more like the kind that Socrates had; after all, we are told, by Joan Didion, that Faulkner heard voices, in writing)—

Who better, to help steer the concept into *our* awareness; i.e., the Earth's? How so? But we'll return to this.

Where was it stored? Or was it? Probably in something abstract, like a conviction. But since everything, brought out, had energy behind it, this recurring action, expressing a conviction, had its energy counterpart. *Only, we couldn't measure it. We couldn't even find it.*

We didn't know where to look.

The only way to deal with it—being more convinced in its convictions than your conviction—was to first root it out. You had to transform it.

Go ahead. Try. It was more stubborn. It was composed of something, more stubborn than you. It had only this that kept it alive. So you HAD TO. You HAD TO. Root the thing out and transform together.

Now, that was the only thing to do. But how?—and of course how so?—until you understood what caused it to hide out and coop up like that. And that those actions it exhibited in the person so struck by it—that those demonstrations clearly proved that somewhere in the energetic structure of the body, it hid out. It came out. It held in its energy the single thing: it was aware.

The moment when it once and forever could not go on. Because it *understood*. It was sprung life-size into birth, FULLY aware. This was its place, where it would remain, invisible. Indicating that the particular life had no great distance it could go, held on a leash, which met it eventually in any direction it set out. Unless gone past by transformation.

Taking the concept of energy awareness, we can raise our own conceptual awareness. Thereby raising our intelligence, in fact.

Such awareness as he wrote about might be an obsession. The character was on the lookout for it. Up ahead. So repetitive as to be almost (but only almost) as if a replication of itself, though in fact rather continuous, never far away. Thus, it would lead us, right up to the hiding places of energy itself. Where it went. Prove to ourselves that it literally hid in *bodies of energy*, in probably *measurable containers of it.* Just like the characters, who (being not very mental) became more or

233

less obsessed, in his work. As we go into hidden streams that energy pursues. And how then it might, in fact, have hidden chakras for itself. Well, we will just speak in such terms. Awaiting better vocabulary, as we go over the facts and details of the case that came to his attention, Faulkner's, as we brought it to him and asked for a few words.

Elsasser, on Bergson's *Matter and Memory* (Bergson agrees with him): "that the observational data show no evidence whatsoever for the existence of a storage mechanism in the brain.

"Bergson exemplifies this [lack of storage mechanism] by comparing the brain with a telephone exchange (the nearest thing, undoubtedly, to a computer that was known at that period). He says that in the human brain as in a telephone exchange there are innumerable wires coming in, innumerable wires going out, . . . but there is no evidence anywhere of a mechanism that would store and at a later time release, information."

> Bergson's model . . . needed therefore to be built up into a genuine theory which embodies the concept of *memory without storage* . . .

However, the obstacles were immense, "largely in the mental attitude of biologists":

> *Here, for the first time in history the biologist has to face squarely his own epistemological problems:* They are condensed in the phrase, "memory without storage."* The advantage of the physicist, which consists in having a long tradition in attacking and ultimately solving epistemological problems, cannot be gainsaid. . . Now it is the biologist's turn . . . It should become clear from the preceding chapters that we must here interpret "memory" in a broad sense, comprising

---

*This phrase might be a pickup, a nutshell example of a similar instance of TRANSPORTING AN IDEA. Even, connected to the other, "action at a distance"—that is, one object or action bearing on another *without* any physical contact with it—a parallel instance inside the same type. But it was gravity to the rescue. It would provide the connection. Gravity, as it affected tiny particles, then led to relativity, and now look, we are bold and brave enough (are we?) to step over another disconnected activity—"memory without storage."

Or is it that with Elsasser's explanations, it is palatable and makes

not only cerebral memory but all information stability in the organism that does not yield to an understanding in terms of mechanistic models. (Elsasser, pages 86–88, my italics)

Now, this was certainly *up Faulkner's alley.** One thing his characters had was memory. In the whole history of literature. Characters often had memory, for that matter. But his did. One thing no one could subtract from DUE TO THE DRIVE OF THE MEMORY.

Because it stopped the character, made it wait—for the action. We just proffer that this stopped, rooted-in-the-ground *tableau*, of the fateful event en route and the character knowing it (allied with the approaching event or the awareness that it had just occurred), in a sense created an energy combination between what was to happen and/or what had happened, through the energy stored in the awareness, wherever it was.

Somebody had to know about this. Somebody knew about this. But the speaking-out mechanism—that didn't yet get added in to the Earth consciousness to create its own awareness of things like this. In this case, parts of the Earth conscience were stored like this. In the awareness "cubicle" or "modules," or then, more psychological terms. The Earth didn't "get it," that where there was reaction such as this, awareness such as this, *there was sure to be energy.*

---

sense, this concept of "memory" that is STORED NOWHERE THAT WE KNOW? Ah-ha.

* That is, it suddenly looked as if cause/effect could go in both directions—that it could be cause/effect/cause (i.e., that the *effect* created a new cause; i.e., was active, not just passive, even if in a dormant mode for a period or also if instant). And that this is necessarily true; i.e., that whoever sees an effect or takes charge of one had very well better look into what new cause is simultaneously being moved into the future, closer into the entry point it has in time. BECAUSE everything is shifted when the effect gets into place. Everything now has to rebalance, so the effect, stopping its drive to become an effect, can quickly pass its energy toward *the thing it left out*, which is now on the road TO BEING CAUSED.

Now, clearly, I suddenly see this as an effect, looking into the thing overlooked, not taken into account, setting it into the cause position in the energy mode. Taken just a little higher, it would be seen to be awareness, and in that moment could become A CAUSE TO CHAMPION.

And often in this sequence, the connections, overlooked, cause great wars and disputes. No one saying: "But look, this is not a dispute but a correction, a rearrangement, a continued search." I hope this is clear.

And you better believe that it was stored. Sometimes, you said, in an archetype. But his characters went one better.

Now, we should know, from the concept of repression, from the sight of a tamped-down container (a volcano, an oil spout), how the pressure built. Where there was no release. So in the milder form but just as stuck, Faulkner's characters *carried their pressurized situation*. And no release came till the event occurred. All the while that *expectation drove them toward it or kept them from stepping out of the way*. From releasing themselves. So this was memory stored inside a human pressurized container. Now that he thought about it, it figured.

Up to this point, I thought I had things under control. This morning, I woke up weary. In a case like that, I bring someone else out to speak. Some people might call her the inner child. Anyway, she knows how to take the stress away. She'll speak to you directly:

> I'm in the most peculiar position possible. I'm getting to be a pioneer. That's the way it feels. Now what would you do? Well, of course you couldn't refuse. Wouldn't want to. Would you? But imagine if people said the things you took for granted were far-fetched. And they for one had never seen such things? And furthermore, they COULD NOT exist?
>
> Now, talk about the temptation to inflation. What was I to say? That yes, me and God were doing this together? Or that after all, it was me? Or what if I up and brought in L, rbC, Q, etc.? Admitted to their presence and hand (ha) in this? For some few in science now defined the measurements of energy in my apartment by my RNG work as measuring feats that only God could carry through. Well, of course that was true. But what were they saying?
>
> That then the energy I was using, was demonstrating, was a demonstration of God? Well, this was really not cartesian. Or was it exactly cartesian? That they lifted things out—if this much out of the ordinary—into a category (dualism offshoot, I guess).
>
> And they said they had it figured out. Either it was impossible (their assumption), or they would ascribe it to God.

Well, I tell you. What a kind of predicament for a person to find herself in. I speak for myself. I have the spirit of a child. Now, imagine if all the grown-ups told you they had never seen anything like you. And furthermore, they knew quite clearly what was possible. And *you were not*. Short of, of course, bringing God into the picture. So shape up or ship out.

But what kind of defense would you have if you said God did it. Well, you had to consider everything. Was this a suggestion they were giving you? Suppose you suddenly began to claim that God had shown you, in a vision, that this was what he planned to do? Well, maybe that was the better way to explain it. That I had been given this to do. As a solemn order.

✖

So I had now been declared impossible. Now I was having me, and it was impossible to accept that I could be born. But why did I feel weary? I think I had tapped into our past.

I went into the timelines of this too. Of all the rejected things that the world was not ready for. That it expelled without even viewing. Obviously, pioneers all went through this. What was the big deal? So I pulled myself together, but if I paid attention to the emotion back there, I felt that weariness. Probably because it was so deep, where this issue was lodged in Human Nature.

Well, this was where St. Paul came in. He knew what to do with doubt.

Also, when you found yourself in a miracle. Because folks said it couldn't happen. And then it happened to *you*. You had gone right outside their vision. They couldn't see you anymore. Pull yourself together.

Reaching into that vision of him struck down.

One of the main forms St. Paul brought in went unnoticed. He brought in the concept of the pressure point—of "having it out" at the first instant it appears.

Of *choosing sides now and forever*. Because all the energy of decision, of processing—the subtle energy, the unconscious positioning— *rushes* TO THE ONE POINT. Then one cannot stand still. Unless, like him, struck dumb. He cannot get up again before DECIDING.

So this is a process, an initiatory secret. Once decided, there is no turning back. There is clarity in view, no matter if even part of oneself ever doubts. The matter *has been concluded*. One knows where one's actions will lead. This might be called "throwing the gauntlet," even if the gauntlet thrown down is from the "higher self." All pressures RUSH to the attacked position, and to survive means to be transformed. If to stand again, to stand in a different position. For the pressure-point procedure is the anathema of doubt.

It attacks all sides and arguments, *on the instant*. All slain. The same is true of pain. If one even skins the knee and lies on the ground, with the focus (automatic) at that point of wound, then all the healing ability from within RUSHES to the wounded area.

This procedure can be a tiny trickle of the old self, following into another millennium, acting automatically, in this tiny cameo reenactment of the Great Moment. But it is that all forms and sizes of the reenactment will draw forth the sudden instinct that survived, being born, in its former EXPERIENCE. No cell that belongs to one's future can escape THE MEMORY, in any version in which it presents or encounters itself. Or if it does, it is the essential encounter, and something will return it to THIS INSTANT. A reflex now. I know, because it struck me that way—eventually, in later years, when even a scrape of a knee would thrust me down, in instinct, not to rise till all the pain was conquered.

If people would say, "Get up," I would not understand what they were talking about. Didn't they know, that when struck down—when any point received a physical blow of pain—to stay with it, not moving, till the light had restored the balance, and the pain simply disappeared? Not to return, because one FACED

IT DOWN, THEN, in its first arrival? This relic or fragment, unrecognizable as a bone of that moment, could be recognized, by its strength of conviction that this was the form such an encounter necessitated. That knowledge brought with it. I had called it Buddhist. Blake knew it. The quantum mind knew it. Doubt disintegrated.

But wasn't it this, a little paradigm and cameo of that, rolled up in the intuition, that came NOW, not before, that when wounded, struck by pain, thrust down with even a knee scrape, stay put. To go into awareness, to shut the rest of the brain off, to let this instinct, even the instinct of a memory, of learned wisdom—the St. Paul moment—even if not brought on, this time by The Light, but beckoning to it—tell the body NOT TO MOVE. Then, as at the moment of myself at the piano, in unmoving stillness except for the racing fingers, the listening mind—in that position, the wisdom of All Time tells the body what to do. Concentrate on receiving the healing, rushing to the point of wound. It must be so. Make it so.

Goswami calls the collapse of the mind material, under the impact of observation by the brain—he never brings up this experience, but the theory he puts forth can be made to fit. Elucidates it. Yes, we will apply it—Brain QM.

Brownian motion (*Einstein: A Life in Science*, page 82)

Einstein wrote a 1905 paper on the behavior of molecules that was convincing to scientists.

> In this paper, it will be shown that according to the molecular-kinetic theory of heat, bodies of microscopically visible size suspended in a liquid will perform movements of such magnitude that they can easily be observed in a microscope, on account of the molecular motions of heat.

But Brownian motion it was. This paper clinched it. That meant—because their activity was visible—these little particles, invisible though they were, existed. We saw *their movement*: what they did. It had to be accounted for somehow. Surely it was not another of these "invisible"/without contact causes that here, in this case, did not even exist. No, this proved they existed. At least, that much was "real." Not forever, but we will leave it at that.

> It is one thing to say, as some nineteenth-century scientists did, that Brownian motion might be explained, in general terms, as the result of the impact of molecules on the suspended particles. It is quite another to *calculate*, as Einstein did, the precise statistical nature of the impact of very large numbers of molecules with suspended particles, and to use that calculation to predict the precise nature of the zigzagging Brownian motion that would result. (page 83)

For instance, HAD JESUS NOT DIED. *If he had lived to a hundred,*

What would he have said?

Taught?

Would he have taken the whole planet and shifted it? Leaned it this way, leaned it that? And in a snap of a finger, showed us more of the consciousness we, as with a transplant liver, rejected? We had to, though. We wanted to "think for ourselves." That meant *we did not want him—or anyone—to think for us. The Earth, in that moment, established its tendency at this moment. And, I now see, perhaps there was some method to the madness of it. Crucify him in order that we might think for ourselves. Not me, but the vast majority. Unconscious, I have to keep saying.*

He saw the alignment; and that on this day, when the alignment reached now, he would be in an alignment that we could know more of him, as knowing (naturally) more of our possible—emphasis "possible"—(one future, one choice): SELF. And why we would have held to our obstinacy to "do it ourselves." But wouldn't he have? Didn't he? Of course.

That is, follow such notions as "To thy own self be true."

How connect humanity on those levels it knew not "the Way to"? But if you could see it, you could see it trying to get to, unconsciously, some HOOK UP WITH—. A threshold just off the horizon. Some place of—call it High Alertness, Awareness—where our intuition was, our "good angels" were.

Every event can be seen atomistically. But for events to combine they either have to be left alone to relate. Or we have to help do it for them.

This multiplication, by connection, was what the sat guru Dhyanyogi-ji meant when he said God is in each person's heart; what happens depends on who's driving.

Dhyanyogi-ji said that nothing is created by humanity that did not exist.

Neither is anything that exists killed.

Light, a photon, emitted when an electron is in an electromagnetic field, when it leaves the event where it is clearly active, reaching another event, can find itself atomistically ignored; in which case leaving the illumination blocked in an apparent enclosure, taken to have no connections at all—no rescue in that direction, for it's a single-location situation or force.

Or we can realize that another view is connecting or revealing the potential. Not to be trapped like a June bug in a jar. This multiplication by amplification depends on there being knowledge in the light.

Using time, to enter events at the time of greatest or smallest effect. This time sensor adds mass as well.

For the smallest thing on Earth to bring about a giant effect, it has to create more energy than it began with. How can small energy know the way to multiply the energy effect? How can it know how to combine in just the way that does? We call it ACCIDENT.

But behind accident is systematic movement toward the moment when the small in number or size is suddenly over the borderline, where it meets REINFORCEMENTS. It is in the tie-breaking vote. The instant off guard. How does time create such pressure spots, sites??? How in fact does it create opportunity? To connect through a line of light, one opportunity touching on another, was the way of creating abundance. Did it "just happen"? No.*

Or then, you say, the little—in its first instant of life—ball-size universe—yes, that's a fact; you could have picked it up and tossed it around, played catch with it!—just by accident expanded into the immeasurably gargantuan universe it turned into when it "grew up."

---

* Also, of course, if Einstein "skipped over the question of "ether," made irrelevant, then (what we are trying to get to, to ask, to imply): was it this very skipped-over thing, discounted, left out, that had to be gone back to? Now armed with what we knew, based on what he retrieved from the total unconscious of all our minds, the total unconscious, as it was willing to yield something up? Then. But not everything. AND based on beginning where he did, leaving, by that "token," out the whole Eastern understanding of "ether," but that would have made unsteady the whole "boatload" of information. And so it steadied itself as it landed here on Earth and made ready the "sails" for yet one more journey, of bringing insight to Life. Yours and mine.

&11L

From Paul Davies, *The Fifth Miracle* (page 62):

We now need to explain . . . the origin of information. Whereas it is good science to seek a physical process to generate matter, it is regarded as unscientific in the extreme to entertain a process that generates information. *Information is not something that is supposed to come for free (like cosmic matter), but something you have to work for.*

Now, that's a thought: *Information is not something that is supposed to come for free (like cosmic matter), but something you have to work for.* But suppose it IS free, though you may still need to work to find how it fits together because, perhaps, it is in your own mind, your own sense of connections, that it fits together. That it "lands," as it were. Inspired. Ready to be "thought" or, put humbly, to "serve." Often thought, put instantly to "jail."

This is really just the second law of thermodynamics revisited, because the spontaneous appearance of information in the universe would be equivalent to a reduction of the entropy [disorder] of the universe—a violation of the second law, a miracle. Now, the fact that the universe contains information is undeniable (because it is not in thermodynamic equilibrium). If information can't get made, it was there at the beginning, as part of the initial input. The conclusion we are led to is that the universe came stocked with information, or negative entropy, from the word "go."[15]

What do astronomical observations say about the information content of the early universe? Here we make a very curious discovery. One of the most compelling pieces of evidence for the big-bang theory is the existence of a universal background of heat radiation, which seems to be a sort of afterglow of the universe's fiery birth. (*Fifth Miracle*, page 62)*

This contradiction is resolved, qualified: "it comes from a careful study of gravitation." (page 63)

---

* "In relativity theory, information pops up again, but in a very different, and very curious, context. It is often said that the theory of relativity forbids anything to travel faster than light. This is not true. It does permit particles to travel faster than light (such theoretical particles are called tachyons). What is forbidden by the theory is the transmission of *information* faster than light." (Bohm, *Wholeness and the Implicate Order*, page 66):

It is significant to point out here that the root of the theory of relativity was probably in a question that Einstein asked himself when he was fifteen years old: "What would happen if one were to move at the speed of light and look in a mirror?" Evidently one would see nothing because the light from one's face would never reach the mirror. This led Einstein to feel that light is somehow basically different from other forms of motion.

From our more modern vantage point, we can emphasize this difference yet more by considering the atomic structure of the matter out of which we are constituted. If we went faster than light, then, as a simple calculation shows, the electromagnetic fields that hold our atoms together would be left behind us (as the waves produced by an airplane are left behind it when it goes faster than sound). As a result, our atoms would disperse, and we would fall apart. So it would make no sense to suppose that we could go faster than light.

Now, a basic feature of the classical order and measure of Galileo and Newton is that one can in principle catch up with and overtake any form of motion, as long as the speed is finite. However, as has been indicated here, it leads to absurdities to suppose that we can catch up with and overtake light. (London & New York: Ark Paperbacks, 1980/1988, pages 122–123)

.If there are patterns, are there not weavers of them? We are *missing some archetypes.*

V

The struggle to get through the last pages of Vol. IV, *Love in Transition* (the one which had the big gap, the pileup at the End, that broke through into the *Space Encounters* books) taught me a lot; it finally dawned on me: the material I was resisting printing, but also resisting "killing," that I recognized as trancelike but not related at all to the present me, had in being passed through, produced a different state of consciousness, at the opposite pole of who I now was.

"Art & Life: A Menippean Paean to the Flea; or, Did Dostoevsky Kill Trotsky?" (*Selected Writings of Milton Klonsky*, page 233)

> For if ever anyone can be said to have been gifted with "second sight" it was surely William Blake. From early childhood, apparently, he had discovered and cultivated within himself the astonishing power (what parapsychologist F. W. Myers once described in the chomping phrase "psychorrhagic diathesis") of envisioning images of such intensity that they were projected before him as apparitions. He could as soon have doubted their real existence as, say, anyone could doubt the reality of his dreams in the course of dreaming them [lucid dreams excepted]. "What seems to Be, he wrote," Is, to those to whom / It seems to be." This was of course Blake's own conscious poetic re-vision of Bishop Berkeley's idealistic conception of being: *esse est percipi* ("to be is to be perceived"); but it was also, it seems to us, a reaffirmation, independently and unconsciously arrived at, of [Christopher] Smart's primitive "cubist" point of view.
>
> By Blake's time, however, the idea of ghosts lingered on only as the ghost of an idea that had already been exorcised by reason, no longer worth considering, though it still might haunt the minds of religious cranks and/or lunatics. Which is in fact how Blake was regarded by many of his contemporaries.

The me that I did "discover" was a humorous, ironic, surrealistic "thinker," who made use of the absurdity of the darkness of total blankness ahead to encounter the emotions of absurdity and fed on Kafka, Nabokov, the surrealists—introduced me to a state of perception where a detachment sat over the material and curiosity was the main ingredient of the mind that wrote or read. I loved this new character and did not identify with the earlier. This one had a secret. The blankness ahead gave it its power. It was verified. Given work to do. It was a medicine I discovered, this me. Part of myself, taught and brought to me.

Let me insert as a Bulletin to the Reader (the year 2000): it seems to start internally. I might "explode" like Vesuvius any minute. I will explain more. It is serious. End Bulletin.

Part
Eight

Chapter Eleven

I am most pleased to be able to stand here on the basis of this writing, as to come in on the basis of other positions or theories would not work. Thus, my birth is an implied one, in that I have a theoretical build-up, a theoretical place in which I might be located.

ɔst pleased to be able to stand in myself,
;. as to come in on the basis of other posit
work. Thus, my birth is an implied one,
buildup, a theoretical place in which I m
did not exist; and so the purpose of the
tion, up to this point—a sidelight of it—w
night have produced a position that
ed as perhaps the result. If the end positi
it would be easy to occupy it. If not, the

And let me tell you, it took me decades to get this implication under my belt, in a solid, unshakable realization.

This place did not exist, and so the purpose of the writing, in part of its intention, up to this point—a sidelight of it—was that perhaps the end might have produced a position that could be hypothesized as perhaps the result. If the end position created such a position, it would be easy to occupy it. If not, there would be no position because one did not exist, there was not enough accumulated focus on the hypothesis—not enough life matter lived inside its question; it did not fit into Earth structures. And thus, through the creation of a personality, a place itself was permitted to exist—that is something that used to exist inside the collective unconscious, where so many of the issues were not settled, as there was not a democracy of settlement, but certain questions monopolized attention. Thus, through the uproar of the inhabitants of the Earth, asking that some of their real problems be addressed, these others, that were in the way, were taken out for problematical attack and enough attention thus given to them that it should be settled once and for all that the energy dispersed through the Earth could allow some o

f   itself
to be

withdrawn from these so popular thought patterns, in order
that the speeders might gather the courage and momentum to not stop at these stoplights but sail through them,
go to places where, these questions already resolved, the
consciousness at a further extreme was relatively practical.
—*Tricks High Up*

�֍

Thus, the medicine I recognized as an internal capacity; not
drawn from, known of, formerly. Yet it did reside there and had
been triggered. I walked around with a secret laugh, in encountering this side of myself, hitherto not known to be so strong
and so SILENT. In what bubbling ethers had he lived? Most
probably, in other people? Is that true? At any rate, the capacity,
the way of thinking, was clearly part of me. Thus did the animus
who had had to stay in the background show me part of the new
consciousness.

This energy now worked on its own material, the inner
fodder that experience threw up. It did not compose in abstrac-
tion. It deduced and deducted and detected and added *back in*
location-correspondence to where I was. It also used the time. It
stretched it into examination tables. It did this gaily. It did this in
perplexity. It did this, ignoring the desperation it could have felt or
the melodrama—except, as said, in the absurd mode, the mode of
contemplation. It was a marriage of circumstance and spirit, and
spirit was equal to the occasion. Joy could speak in this voice. It
defiantly dared outer situations to take that away. It made a private
space, even here. This corresponded to the me of the future, the
energy levels where to feel THIS WAY made a match, and to feel the
other way created heaviness. This one created helium attractions. It
could float in those atmospheres. It could banish the outer circumstances, by strengthening the fort of taking what it had and saying
THIS WILL DO.

So there is nothing to be done for it. The me who was interested in the former pages here is gone. She cannot be retrieved. The things inside this new interest—why, they are ETERNAL. Wrack and ruin all around, it could be that in Universe time, one feels an inexplicable joy and satisfaction. It is Father Time's bag, held back, ready now. And one feels it. The invisible, CHAOTIC future had been followed. Yes, that was it.

Everyone's past. Yes, one has hooked into that. In fact, to one's own self in that pack. THAT self, the chaotic one, the one that had to be slipped into Real Time. That one. Had one found the way to it? Divesting oneself of customary and expected reactions and there-fore routes, accelerating this one, yes,* what would it produce? Positiveness and power—people wanted

---

* Will this lead to anything? We hope so. Divested of other focus, we will secretly follow this pathway that has come to us. Secretly, that is. Each person can reach THEIR OWN SECRETS.

to hear of it. It was in them. It was their right and CURRENCY.*

---

* And so I began to announce a big battle underway. I saw how the state of unconsciousness of the Earth had camouflaged some of its greatest worth..

That what was in the unconscious was a kind of storage or vat, that could be brought out, upon request.

That that request had been activated.

That the Earth had asked that what it did not use before, but stored up, and had no key into, might be shown to it. And in the memory of its valor, its conquests, its defeats, its uses of a particular type of energies, it learn its own universe-system, what kept it circling in the sky, what kept it just short of devastation many times. What it had invested in. Everything, as a matter of fact, *it had* WITHHELD *from itself about itself.*

So as from a father or mother, who finally begins to tell the offspring some of its histories and lineage, for the Earth to learn more of its unconscious wisdom. What was known about it, which I didn't know at all, of course, but from (as a "for instance") these energies that poured in, saying so. Asserting.

A picture of the Earth through the
eyes of a
different consciousness,
call it.
One just as future to it, as
the present "I" was
to the one it
later met (as just described)

Gopi KRISHNA

Kundalini: The Evolutionary Energy in Man
with psychological commentary by James Hillman, pages 12–13:

> During one such spell of intense concentration I suddenly felt a strange sensation below the base of the spine, at the place touching the seat, while I sat cross-legged on a folded blanket spread on the floor. The sensation was so extraordinary and so pleasing that my attention was forcibly drawn towards it. The moment my attention was thus unexpectedly withdrawn from the point on which it was focused, the sensation ceased. Thinking it

to be a trick played by my imagination to relax the tension, I dismissed the matter from my mind and brought my attention back to the point from which it had wandered. Again I fixed it on the lotus, and as the image grew clear and distinct at the top of my head, again the sensation occurred. This time I tried to maintain the fixity of my attention and succeeded for a few seconds, but the sensation extending upwards grew so intense and was so extraordinary, as compared to anything I had experienced before, that in spite of myself my mind went towards it, and at that very moment it again disappeared. I was now convinced that something unusual had happened for which my daily practice of concentration was probably responsible.

I had read glowing accounts, written by learned men, of great benefits resulting from concentration, and of the miraculous powers acquired by yogis through such exercises. My heart began to beat wildly, and I found it difficult to bring my attention to the required degree of fixity. After a while I grew composed and was soon as deep in meditation as before. When completely immersed I again experienced the sensation, but this time, instead of allowing my mind to leave the point where I had fixed it, I maintained a rigidity of attention throughout. The sensation again extended upwards, growing in intensity, and I felt myself wavering; but with a great effort I kept my attention centered round the lotus. Suddenly, with a roar like that of a waterfall, I felt a stream of liquid light entering my brain through the spinal cord.

Entirely unprepared for such a development, I was completely taken by surprise; but regaining self-control instantaneously, I remained sitting in the same posture, keeping my mind on the point of concentration. The illumination grew brighter and brighter, the roaring louder, I experienced a rocking sensation and then felt myself slipping out of my body, entirely enveloped in a halo of light. It is impossible to describe the experience accurately. I felt the point of consciousness that was myself growing wider, surrounded by waves of light. It grew wider and wider, spreading outward while the body, normally the immediate object of its perception, appeared to have receded into the distance until I became entirely unconscious of it. I was now all consciousness, without any outline, without any idea of a corporeal appendage, without any feeling or sensation coming from the senses, immersed in a sea of light simultaneously conscious and aware of every point, spread out, as it were, in all directions without any barrier or material obstruction. I was no longer myself, or to be more accurate,

no longer as I knew myself to be, a small point of awareness con-
fined in a body, but instead was a vast circle of consciousness in
which the body was but a point, bathed in light and in a state of
exaltation and happiness impossible to describe.

Amit Goswami, pages 44–45:

I accompanied a mystic friend, Joel Morwood, to Ojai to hear
the famous spiritual teacher, Krishnamurti speak. . . .
"So is the brain of the observer prior to consciousness, or is it
consciousness prior to the brain?' [Joel asked afterwards.]
I could see Joel's trap. "I am talking about consciousness as
the subject of experiences."
"Consciousness is prior to experiences. It is without an object
and without a subject," Joel said.
"Sure, that's vintage mysticism . . ."
But Joel was not to be intimidated . . . "Your scientific blinders keep you from understanding. Underneath, you believe that
consciousness can be understood by science, that consciousness
emerges in the brain, that it is an epiphenomenon. Comprehend
what the mystics are saying. Consciousness is prior and uncondi-
tioned. It is all there is. There is nothing but God."
The last sentence suddenly triggered a turnabout in my thinking. I suddenly realized that consciousness *is* the ground of all
being, what the Uphanishadic *rishis*, or seers, had called Brahman.
If consciousness is the ground of all being, then matter exists as
possibilities within consciousness. And consciousness chooses
among the available possibilities by recognizing a particular one
for a particular event.
When you look at a gestalt picture of double meaning, . . . [t]
he possibility is already there; you are just recognizing it.
To avoid dualism we must turn materialist metaphysics on
its head. Matter is not the ground of being, as Feynman asserted.
(pages 44–45)

wait, I shouted
wait
make it clear here
TELL THE READERS
this isn't
only about me
I winced at all the pages squashed by the computer-PK, indignant
BUT
always looking for the consciousness
even in the apparent wreck
then I understood
clearings were like this
Let Faulkner speak

It's about
before it happened, IF
IF *it didn't happen*
IF IT DID
what could be seen IF THIS COULDN'T
it's about
your total self, your relative self,
relative to
POSSIBILITIES NOW
solutions

it's about FRIENDS
you forgot
or never met
it's about
totality
universality
it's about
the Earth now
it's about
YOU, *folks*
it's about
all the times it began something
archetype of the Alpha–Omega
Jesus beginning–end
the Angelic realm, host of angels, when they
"bring something to the finish"
It's about the ancient A's
from different Alphabets.
FROM THE SAME—
about your mission, the one you've announced, how I heard about it,
THE UNIVERSE DID
It's about you
What you dream and what

———————————————

your soul dreamed for you
it's about
the time to finish
A plus, and the next letter, it's
THE END

Mother and Father of the Universe
completing a cycle
with us
that's right,
it's also about
YOU and YOU and YOU TOO, *that little sentence you almost said, that the wind*
picked up
WHY *it meant*
so much
and why digging deep you might find an IN
TIRE
unit
To compete with
finally, you compete
only, you don't call it that
because this level
doesn't "compete"
it complements
yes, compliments,
it completes

264

> Sacred mysticism recognizes the transformation of percep-
> tion not as a separate visual experience . . . In alchemy the
> stage was referred to as the peacock's tail in which "eyes"
> unfurled amid some of the most royally blazing colours
> known in nature. (Gopi Krishna, *The Evolutionary Energy in
> Man*, page 202)

Peacock's tail eyes—that's what visions were. And how they related to the Larger Picture they were in.

I have mentioned how Gopi Krishna described, about twelve years after his first major mystical experience, he sank into a "condition of exaltation and self-expansion similar to . . . the very first occasion, in December 1937." To pick up on that story, the roaring of the waterfall was replaced this time by "a cadence like the humming of a swarm of bees, enchanting and melodious; and the "encircling glow" was now "a penetrating silvery radiance, already a feature of my being within and without." He continued:

> The marvelous aspect of the condition lay in the sudden
> realization that although linked to the body and surround-
> ings I had expanded into a titanic personality, conscious
> from within of an immediat-

e

contact with an intensely conscious universe, a wonderful inexpressible immanence all around me. My body, the chair I was sitting on, the table in front of me, the room encircled by walls, the lawn outside and the space beyond including the Earth and sky, appeared to be most amazingly mere phantoms in this real, interpenetrating and all-pervasive ocean of existence which, to explain the most incredible part of it as best I can, seemed to be simultaneously unbounded, stretching out immeasurably in all directions, and yet no bigger than an infinitely small point. From this marvelous point the entire existence, of which my body and its surroundings were a part, poured out like radiation, as if a reflection as vast as my conception of the cosmos were thrown out upon infinity by a projector no bigger than a pinpoint, the entire intensely active and gigantic world picture dependent on the beams issuing from it. The shoreless ocean of consciousness in which I was now immersed appeared infinitely large and infinitely small at the same time, large when considered in relation to the world picture floating in it and small when considered in itself, measureless, without form or size, nothing and yet everything.

It was an amazing and staggering experience . . . I was intensely aware internally of a marvelous being so concentratedly and massively conscious as to outlustre and outstature infinitely the cosmic image present before me, not only in point of extent and brightness but in point of reality and substance as well. The phenomenal world, ceaselessly in motion characterized by creation, incessant change, and dissolution, receded into the background and assumed the appearance of an extremely thin, rapidly melting layer of foam upon a substantial rolling ocean of life, a veil of exceedingly fine vapour before an infinitely large conscious sun. (pages 207–208)

Bulletin: Who has the intensity
that pushes me to the borderline of bearability—that
seems to come
from inside me
must not say a word
no contact outside
Not dangerous, except if you care about the impressions you make
on people
such as if you walk up to them as Vesuvius
This is a new situation,
Aug. 31, 2000
Bulletin ended

I could compare other Augusts. Yes. But that's only part of it. Am I
being "enlightened?" Is the energy coming to get me?
So the reader must keep straight two caves
the one where I am exploding, that is not a real cave,
and the real cave, that has been determined not a real cave either,
in Romania,
where it is known to have been—a monastery
—cave to me, though
in all appearances
Bulletin ended again.

Picked back up:
We will soon have to learn to quanti-

fy them,

the Caves,
all supra-extraordinary
the third
the Cave of Realization
of a Yogi
and not only one
resided in a cave
We could add others
in the great history of caves
in India
we could go to Jerusalem
we will see how many our revelation
shows to us
or just stop, in mentioning
that these deserve
MENTION TOO
Bulletin now definitively stopping exploding
we return to text*

---

* For some time past, I had wondered if someone, some ones, was/were making a "BOW"; i.e., if someone (someones) were at what WE CALL Ground Zero. What happens there, I don't know, in a case like this. But were they sending a message FROM IT? Wherever it was. I took it down dutifully. Suppose it came from there. The intensity said SOMETHING OF THE SORT. More soon to be known.

Often now my brain was virtually past the point where my mind could reason. Some kind of intensity overload. That's why I shouldn't speak. It was something energetic or chemical. As if your BRAIN got adrenaline. OR ALL OF THE BLOOD RUSHED TO YOUR HEAD. You had cut your wrist somehow. But it was your head. And the brain didn't understand how to process in this manner. It was supposed to be sent oxygen. What was this that was happening to it? IT couldn't breathe so well like this. IT COULDN'T BREAK THINGS DOWN.

273

*rbc

NEW BULLETIN:

We have learned to *follow our eyes*.
Now we have to
learn to

FOLLOW OUR ENERGY!!!

I hated to just break in like that, announcing it so bluntly. But it seemed to be what I was DISCOVERING. What was the Earth *facing into*??*

What was not said was how many attachments, *memories, the Earth had generated—felt out there in the universe, as it received, spread, distributed the waves of it.* That is, in its atmospheres, where it stretched in distances it could carry such energy through.

The type that was sustaining, that one looked back to.

How much of this the Earth had bred. It had contributed "LOCATION."

Not easily forgotten. Not in the complexity that such gifts were created. And so the Earth HAD TIES.

As wildfires brought this news to me, I tried to keep focus. Receiving these new, forming "information bits" as they went out from the universe into the Earth spectrum. September 2, 2000. To continue.

---

* The printer had decided it knew better what to print and what size it should be. And I didn't have any say in the matter.

Now my brain was being OVERruled. YES. OVER-
ruled by energy it could never hope to master. energy torrents, finding a windowpane inside to stand behind and watch, or—

It was exactly the situation
that made one say
"I lost my head."
LOST MY HEAD, FOLKS

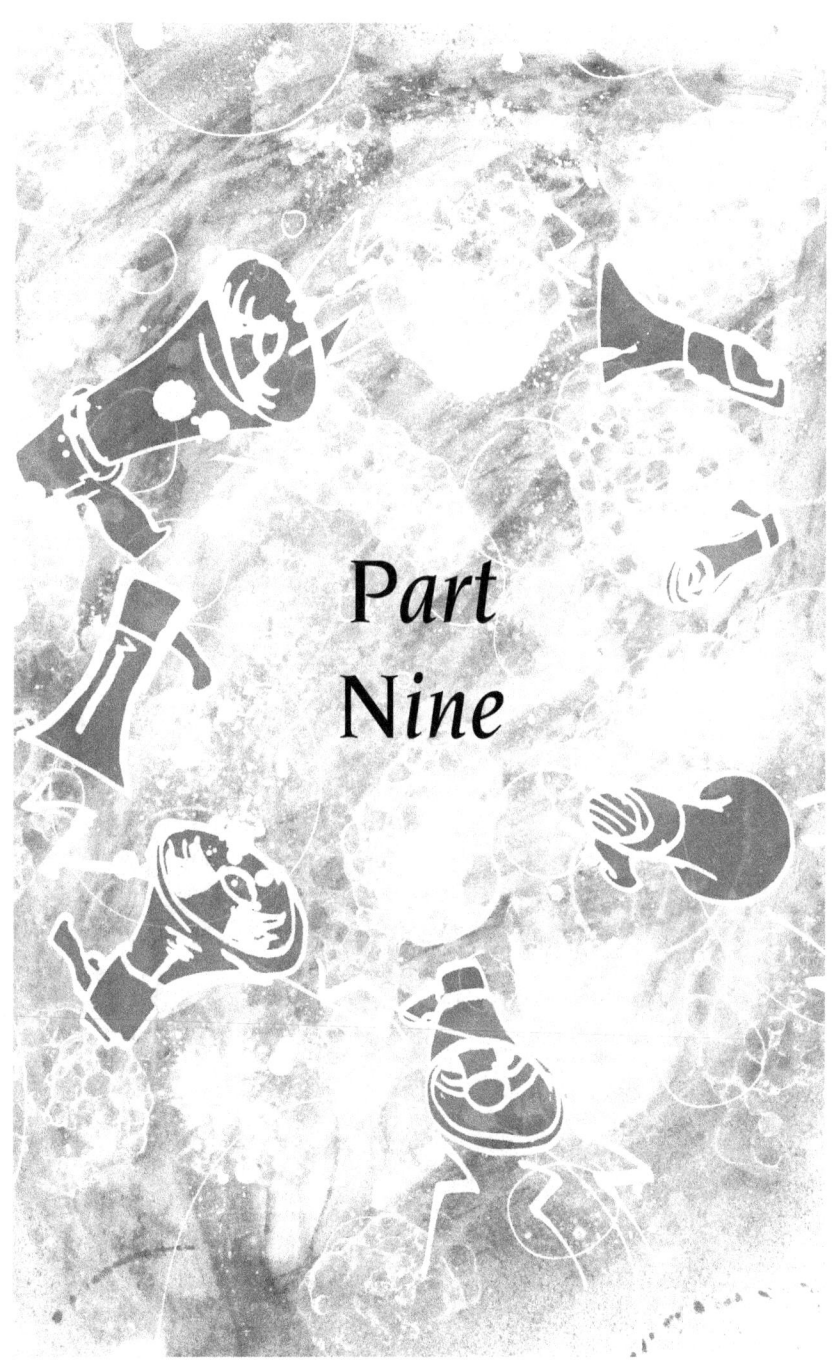

Part
Nine

Chapter Twelve

Shall we open the journal in an advanced page and then quickly flip backwards?

Just so, in the past, such consciousness had been willing to break itself down, to see what would be the result. But we will not linger in this. It is a process up ahead. And we are not there yet. In fact, as we flip backwards, we see that we are in total oblivion to where we are. We have no clue at all. And so let us start and find out how we found out,

if we did. Of course, we know that we did. But that is not even assured, as we go through the steps once more. Because anything can happen at each re-stepping into the past, even merely in the reading of it, as each mind that joins it contributes, even going backward into what has already finished, parting time in that mind, recombining in that mind and finding out how and what the fin-ished result might be, from over there. No, this is in truth how such things work. I do not exist, although I have made myself exist in this fashion, but once again do not, in order to.

The hypothesis is I must be somewhere at any instant, at every instant. Who would I be in this instant? Where would I be? I would be everywhere, it goes without saying. But where could I wake myself up?

Where would my primary concern be to find myself? Of course, that would be in particular places if I had a name or did not have a name. But where could I match these concerns with a location? I could establish the degree of energy I would leave behind when alive. Then find that degree of energy turned toward these concerns I would find in myself, not alive.

And where the match was, the nonalive me would try to force its way into the alive me, or an alive me, a location, that is, where the concerns could reside, without there being too much conflict to say that there was harmony and respect, intention. In other words, that this was primarily me. Or a primary me. And therefore one could proceed into the next instance. Otherwise, one could stay in this instant, calling it time, stretching it, examining it. But if one reached the conclusion that this answer had been reached, one could call time in, tell it to *move, merely because the issues had moved significantly.* This is how real time moves. And universally has form. This is the universal form of *movement.* Time is only p

L

racticing to be time when it does

conclude. But real time does not call itself time without being connected to eternity. So time that is called time is merely the hypothetical location of issues in eternity when they are more loosely or less intensely connected to it. When they hypothesize themselves rather than realize themselves.

Able to realize myself and not hypothesize myself, I set before myself some of my own concerns in this journal, supposing I did not exist, which in some way I did not during this journey. But in all significant ways, I did. For I *knew I would reach myself, preexisting and asking myself to ask these questions, in its own words and ways.*

It could delete itself a thousand times, en route, *provided it did not delete me. Or in order not to delete me.* And in fact the consciousness that implied. But only *implied*—in the journey. There was no guarantee I existed, from its point of view, which from my point of view was the only guarantee that I existed. *And that perhaps this was a form of me.*

Of course, I knew the answer But that was not existence. Only knowing. But supposing it existed, it would pass these tests—which were the way consciousness grows: if finding itself in situations like this has no choice but to grow—that is, express new faces and forms of what it already is. Or is only because it acts in the only way it would if it were. So from here, found in being rather than that already confirmed final fact. Unmoving and unquestioned. A name. A place. A position.

I challenged my own mind to accept me. This is how it was.

bC

Now, who this "I" is has no relevance whatsoever at this point, not in the context it exists in. Inside the context, relative to the Earth it has been implied. And that is all that matters. That was the purpose, to get the implication so strong from within the structures of the brain of the first person, *which is myself*, who encountered it, affronted it, it would be able to win out as the most logical, or only logical, conclusion. Thus, it was the victory of a pathway cut through the normal lines of communication of the brain. It was the mind itself trying to speak through the dead ends and dead lines, electricity lines that no longer knew what electricity was or how to carry it. They had forgotten.

Thus, as there had been agreed that it is proper to carry out investigations from within and collections of books, that such conclusions have merit, it has been carried out here, using the same or similar kinds of evaluations but with the matter under investigation being the human soul.

2024

Reading this . . . it's real to me. Perhaps it's a fantasy?

A fantasy? Do you think that? Now? After everything?

No, that's it. I don't. Reading it now, I fall into it. I read it sacredly, as if having found a record, a history, of something that happened, or IS happening right now: like how I got here, like who I really am—written under this stone or IN STONE for me to find. A graveyard I visited and found this relic of me. This information for me to use. This private history. Real history. Something in the making as it was being made, a real mind thinking. A real entity. Is it now me? It's now me. But I didn't know myself when this was me; the me from this point of view now, 2023, knew me because what I wrote came to be. But it was written outside time. That's it. It was Outside 3-D. Here is how I brought myself into 3-D.

Of Newton: Letters to Penelope

The wave having collapsed for some moments, we will see some vital information—skipped.

Newton had already said that attraction increased or decreased in intensities or force. It did this relative to distances and mass.

This topic introduced, we will start here. See more how, quite normally, these attractions work in our lives all the time. That we take for granted, without noticing they are laws with *implications* extending into where we can no longer see. And thus lose all vocabulary—except incredulity, etc. However, we will definitely avoid taking any mystery from the Earth, only shifting the locations of it.

We will not be at a loss, as formerly. That being at a loss meant something had built to an unacceptable degree. But we did not have the capacity to put it into words "Time Entrapment." Trapping us like mice, etc., if we let it. And so we start here. Or stop here. To be picked up. Further on.

NEWTON: *Opticks*
(New Britannica Encyclopaedia: Macropaedia, 15th ed., vol. 23)

Pages 893–894:

> Beginning with Kepler's *Paralipomena* in 1604, the study of optics had been a central activity of the scientific revolution. Descartes . . .

*rbC

> had added a new mathematical regularity to the science of light, supporting the conviction that the universe is constructed according to mathematical regularities. Descartes had also made light central to the mechanical philosophy of nature; the reality of light, he argued, consists of motion *transmitted through a material medium*. Newton fully accepted the mechanical nature of light, although he chose the atomistic [point] alternative and held that light consists of material corpuscles in motion. The corpuscular conception of light was always a speculative theory on the periphery of his optics, however.
>
> The core of Newton's contribution [to optics] had to do with colours (my italics)

To go further, which he did not at the time . . .

How did the clouds pull up, as if out of a magician's sleeve, the images that materialized as I photographed them in a trance?

Fancy that.

> The sun on falling waters writes the text
> Which yet is in the eye or in the thought.
> It was a hard thing to undo this knot.
> —Gerard Manley Hopkins

Does my mind, seeing something indecisive, "put" the images there? Does "the inconclusive" attract my mind to a mental sketch pad?

Newton did not theorize about my images—what sketched them in my clouds—why? Because he was deep into the focus—complementarity—side of the light, the side that HELD THE FOCUS. The concentration aspect.

But Newton, whom no one could focus better than, nevertheless was sure of his theory: the Light had only one form (not true).

Hold on! Wait! The light, when translated by the photoreceptors in our eyes, results in signals. And our brain says: ah-ha.

What?

Well, it says: ah-ha. The signal, like information from a lighthouse, in this case telling my brain: *Out there, you just saw—red. No, blue. No, here's the signal again. You saw—violet.*

So, what the light is busy bringing to my eyes is—not pictures, but signals. It all comes down to electricity again. The particles carrying, in the electricity in the air, striking my vision, that form of its speech, I, you, all of us, get—know it well: vision.

From Britannica.com, "Isaac Newton: Career of Isaac Newton: The Optics":

> There is no evidence that the theory of colours, fully described by Newton in his inaugural lectures at Cambridge, made any impression, just as there is no evidence that aspects of his mathematics and the content of the Principia, also pronounced from the [Trinity College] podium, made any impression. Rather, the theory of colours, like his later work, was transmitted to the world through the Royal Society of London, which had been organized in 1660. When Newton was appointed Lucasian profession, his name was probably unknown in the Royal Society; in 1671, however, they heard of his reflecting telescope and asked to see it. Pleased by their enthusiastic reception for the telescope and by his election to the society, Newton volunteered a paper on light and colours early in 1672, On the whole, the paper was also well received, although a few questions and some dissent were heard.
>
> *Controversy*. Among the most important dissenters to his paper was Robert Hooke, one of the leaders of the Royal Society, who considered himself the master in optics and hence he wrote a condescending critique of the unknown process . . .
>
> In 1675, during a visit to London, Newton thought he heard

Hooke accept his theory of colours. He was emboldened to bring forth a second paper, an examination of the colour phenomena in thin films, which was identical to most of Book Two as it later appeared in the *Opticks* . . .

In 1704 Newton combined a revision of his optical lectures with the paper of 1675 and a small amount of additional material in his *Opticks*.

A second piece which Newton had sent with the paper of 1675 provoked new controversy. Entitled "An Hypothesis Explaining the Properties of Light," it was in fact a general system of nature. Hooke apparently claimed that Newton had stolen most of the contents from him. And Newton boiled over again . . .

Newton was also engaged in another exchange of his theory of colours with the Circle of English Jesuits in Liege, perhaps the most reveling exchange of all. Although their objections were shallow, their contention that his experiments were mistaken lashed him into a fury. The correspondence dragged on until 1678.[16]

⊠

Short of dating, one cannot say how old the cave monastery Sinca Veche, near Făgăras, Romania, is (a cave whose historical society I was made an honorary member of, so I got a lot of inside details about it on my visits to it). For an underground *Principia*, caves are very apt.

Back then, in the cave, when I visited—

Someone had LEFT THE RESEARCH LAID OUT. As if walking away from a meal, finished just before we arrived, put the pieces one beside the other; we only have to see if/where "they belong."

The tower of the Sinca Veche cave, now fallen, had a tiny aperture, through which light trickled in, landing on the floor, striking the opaqueness, ignominiously dark. In the cave walls are holes that once held giant crystals, reclining, esoteric in purpose. They were stolen in the twentieth century—bringing bad luck to the thief (so say the witnesses). In the mid-twentieth century, playing in the cave, local kids, including a man I met, who became the historical-society president, entered the cave with matches; at first they stayed near the entrance, near the giant crystals. But one day they went further in.

Holding their lit matches, the kids arrived at a chamber, where, etched into the wall is the face of an ancient teacher.

Beside that a yin-yang image—inside a double triangle.

In what period—we are curious—was this image drawn? Why did the cave setting, in which tiny tiny quartz crystals lie on the ground

287

outside, along the foliaged walk,* with the single ray of light dropping to the entrance floor, echo Plato?

AND HOW DID WE DISMISS, SHUT IT OUT? exclude, bar, reduce to tatters the thought of such teachers, who knew (in Greece, following Pythagoras, following Aristotle; in India) millennia ago that the world was

---

*From "ultrasonics" in the Oxford Family Encyclopedia: Piezoelectric crystals, which quartz crystals are, are used in making visible such things as a foetus— through scanners that "send out beams of sound . . . above the range of human hearing . . . [The sound waves] are created by piezoelectric crystals in the handset."

Suddenly this discovery of ultrasound allows for peering right through the wall of an abdomen at an incipient tiny unborn baby. How so? It was only sound waves, we thought—innocents that we were. That when it sounded like sound, well by golly, THAT'S WHAT IT WAS. We reject the theory, of course. We defiantly declare that never in all of future history could sound waves bring to us pictures of the inner physiological self. Defiantly label such an assertion ludicrous, not to say insane. EXCEPT THAT we proved that this was exactly a fact of "Nature."

And you tell me that people who put giant crystals into holes in walls in caves (as in Romania)—hadn't an inkling OF WHAT THEY WERE DOING. And when they said they were "connecting" with the stars by letting a beam of light, through a single hole in the tower, fall onto the floor of the cave (otherwise dark), so as to get a connection with other universes, they HADN'T AN INKLING of how to put crystals and holes-in-towers together to make some sort of system that repercussed; so as to put into their mind, what? Why, they said (we hear) that somehow it instructed their capacity for visions. (No.) Well, just to go to sleep there and that would do it. Rather as Greek worshippers of the god Aesculapius "slept on" an illness in an Aesculapian temple, and—some of them—woke up "healed." Well, in the Romanian cave, they went them one better. They had crystals.

We do not know whether they knew that in Plato, *chained to the wall in a cave, having no direct sunlight*, was a parable about the human condition: faulty vision. And, let me tell you, a lot of people and institutions are responsible for this predicament.

Their crystals, they thought, offered assistance in making them psychic. Some go further today and say, why, this was a cave of extraterrestrials! No? Yes, they say it.

round. Not flat.* And one, c. 230 BC, Aristarchus of Greece, after careful *observation*, speculated that the earth revolved around the sun. And nobody put him on trial.

Eratosthenes, with a stick in the ground and his brain, calculated the Earth's circumference, pretty accurately.

How, surveying the Earth, slide over the things decided not to be visible, using only those of the faculties thus seen with? HOW?

But we started at the end, with *their answers*. We wanted to rediscover what *they knew by intuition*? We wanted to work at the answers, debate them.

WELL, NOW WE HAVE RIGHT AT

---

* To take a side look at how the Early Christian travels are taught in theology schools of Orthodox Christianity—scrutinizing the travels of St. Paul—it is explained that he spoke (in the great open spaces of the Athens theater) of the gods of the Greeks. That he spoke of their philosophers because he knew them. Knew, it is said here (in Romanian theology), of Pythagoras. What did he, the Middle Easterner, with the wide travel, know? Unlike later readers who learned of his letters? But not of these culturally accessible popping seeds of ideas that gave birth to the philosophy of Europe??? Typically, it now seems clear, we receive the IDEAS robbed of the breadth of context—let us say, surrounding esprit—of the person who acted like a womb for them. The founding "father/mother" releases the child (idea/work) into the hands of Mother Earth. But the individual, working in the idea that follows, does not place it in the context of an interconnected planet. Thus reducing it. We do this repeatedly.

Strip and narrow down the context of the gestalt of ideas. Calling it "product of his/her time." Then erasing all but the single "product," denying it roots. He was a Roman citizen. Think of that too. Rome, the ruling power of, as www.history.com, puts it, "continental Europe, Britain, much of western Asia, northern Africa and the Mediterranean islands." This gives a somewhat different portrait—very unlike the fisherman type. Hadn't he studied in a rabbinical school with Gamaliel, who gave us Gamaliel's Principle, warning, says Wikipedia, "the Jewish Sanhedrin against killing Jesus' disciples, saying that if their ideas were of human origin, they would 'come to nought' and the Jews did not need to worry about them; but if they were from God, their ideas would be impossible to overthrow anyway, and if the Jews tried to stop them, they would be fighting against God." And certainly he was not one who poured over a TV and newspapers. Just think of how CLOSE knowledge was to being tested by Life itself, in its laboratories. Are you going to say that life has no laboratories?

So, sure he spoke of miracles. Hadn't he called over and over on them—TO SAVE HIS LIFE? Life was closer to the gut back then. Necessarily.

So if we don't go back and get it accurate, we won't mix and blend ourselves into the PRODUCT of our past. The HOPE of its ideas. But merely a "reduction," that didn't add in context, breadth, depth—things like that

THE END* Of course, for variety, we could end this volume here. Lean, sleek, slender—for balance. SHALL WE END IT HERE? A few nuggets, much to think on. Shall we seek BALANCE, by stopping this volume HERE????

INTO THE MIXTURE.
of
WHO WE ARE.

*We do not say: at the end of what? Everybody can assume it is a millennium. And this become dated. But what if it is SOMETHING ELSE ENTIRELY THIS IS THE END OF. Something not hence BROUGHT "UP." We will try with this hypothesis.

The answer to that question was NO. We will go—just a little—further. Still keeping it slender.

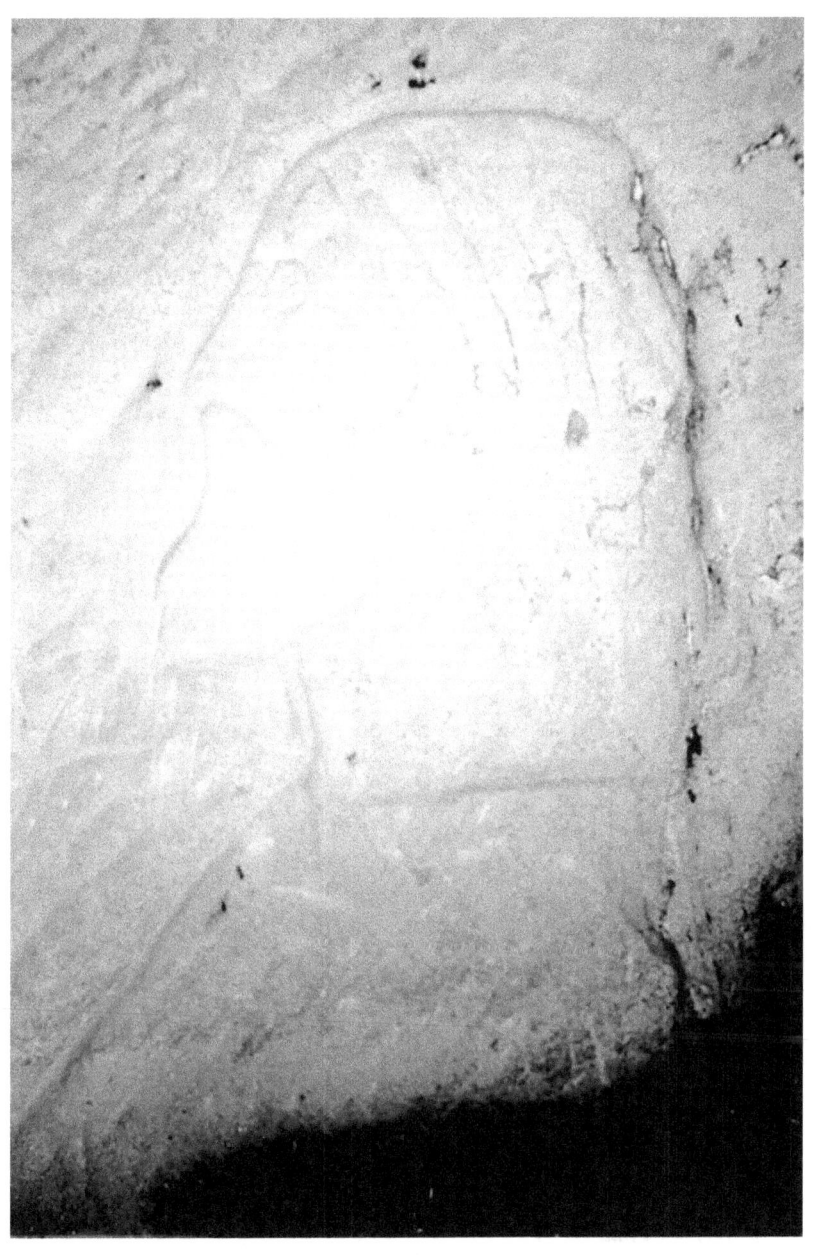

I am here as if having just arrived from another century or even universe, with the feeling of being at least two places at once, completely aware that physically, at least in one physical form, this is where I am and that I have to pay attention to it, but also aware that it is only a place I turn my focus. My focus—basically in another source—can focus here. That my energy, even, is coming from there and of a type that exists there (oh, you hypocrite, you idealizer, but we will see if this is true; for after all, we say things and then find that by some distant light, it is precisely as it would be if we could see that far—which we cannot, we hasten to say. But perhaps the speaker can. "Are you finished now, and can I go on?" that non-present figment of my multiple-character structure asks? OR RATHER, is it no figment at all? as many these days ask and seek to learn)? This is how it feels.

I will find who else is in this mind, who else lives or is or talks to here (we hasten to add we just did). Having been alone for the better part of ???? years, I now find that just as I could have a way to enter the world on a basis of joining, I am moved immediately out of it—into a state of mind where every advantage the new situation brings is only to push me toward this state of being, in fact the one from which the books were written and in which they have meaning. Only, that condition was far from me at the time of writing. A step behind me, in that I could go to it. BUT it was not me there—coming here, in a conscious effort that I must remember where I am. As (in a sense) it now is.

So now, in real science fiction, I don't know how long it will last.

It seems to relate to "clearing the frequencies"; each step taken, each action based on that, carries me further and further—toward what feels like solid ground; for it has understandings I value inside it. And it, moreover, is a completely convincing energy state; FOR— more powerful than the mental state I could bring to question it. No, it is as real as my own mind, as the energy I use to *take steps with my legs*, as the energy I use to think. However, it is in multiple locations, in the very thought processes that are present in it.

NOTES FROM THE END OF THE WORLD

So I am now out in space, in a mental space that is universal in scope and in the energy it uses to think with and create with, for it does create, the answers in actions to things it decides to notice and include as inside and not outside, that ask that that be so or place themselves in the path of it. Is this close to the life form I am? A shape, I guess, that can turn in many faces, or elongate—perhaps with a neck like a giraffe, sticking up above reality with a giraffe's head higher than it. That is, to encompass the situation as if a unity. creating a trail, in search of like species, which of course there are, this is only an initial impression. I stretch the time, creating a me that is wondering, whereas of course there is *knowing* instead. But the wondering is a quality I do create.

I came here, hearing of the photon belt. I stop myself. That's a bit of an exaggeration. Did I? I don't know. But this next isn't. For as much as many are happy to be alive on the Earth at this time, I had the quandary that I had to be here.* And somehow suddenly I have come—here I am—probably in initiation energy, meaning of many—who knew that this would be the way my/their evolution was most facilitated (and hopefully interactively, and it could be retroactively; let us see). And if they ever wanted to give to me—and vice versa—it was in this moment. Like this. I had to come here. So.

---

* I myself did not know why I wrote this. But in the passing year, the reason began to dawn on me, if it could be "carried out." We do not say that it can be. But just suppose that it could.

Now if I can get myself together and get my wits together, I shall make this the start of a new book. Rather: NOW, to start the new book, the book that was waiting uncommenting, holding all of the voice that this is in abeyance. Whatever voice it is, it has never been here before.* Perhaps just in moments.

---

*Some things I recognize, in myself. Take, for instance, how I see Descartes. Something was unsure. That's where it started. He could not take the word of a voice from the past, perused in a book—not "just like that." Without some logic to it.

Check. I'd say that's an OK.

He, then, had the matter brought to deadlock and UNLOCKED right then and there. Without moving.

I do that too. Check.

Now, how I do this is by an old Buddhist principle.

Though I didn't know it, as Descartes didn't. But the universe kept "throwing it down," in various modes. Clues all over the ground. So how I "have it out" is the following. IF I am "struck down"—now, that's an interesting way to say it—if I have a wound (we'll say it this way too), I don't do what I observe all around me: many majorities of people jump straight up and move, talk about it, make a sound, etc. NO. What I have OBSERVED that I do—and eventually wondered why and learned it was taught to Buddhist meditators at some level of their study—is freeze. But I have already mentioned this in the context, as well, as an implied teaching of St. Paul, *the same principle* Descartes used, "TO BECOME SURE." He either just got hit over the head by certainty. Or he felt a huge issue. What to do? HAVE THE MATTER OUT
RIGHT THERE.

I got to the point where I could see the horizons of where I was. And that's when it became clear to me; this was it: "clearing the frequencies." It existed. AND what's more, it would be what I did—so far as I could see—for the rest of my life. Or rather, it would be the NEW THING that impacted me enough, to want to tell the whole Earth about it. In what way they participated, one by one, thinking, even, they lived in isolation. But from the "frequency point of view," they were in its world. Always (everyone) in every moment, not only on solid ground, but IN A FREQUENCY.

EINSTEIN E=

Mass times

Mass,
of concentration,
INCREASES
with focus
UNIFIED
it therefore
INCREASES:

•

NUCLEI.
Attracted
hold together
bind,
solitonlike, a HOLDING
system,
greater mass
attraction—
to THAT FORM.

Amt:
• of energy,
held,
has ability to magnetize
through time. Cross
distances, purely, through
non-shift
of focus. Purely
through
HOLDING FIRM.
NONVARIATION of
gear or
attention. Can be
said to accelerate.
But unaware of the
concept "speed."
Aware of "Likeness,"
"matching vibration,"
"matching" intention.
Completion of mission.
Alpha/
Omega.

This is called

(or based on)
The CERTAINTY
PRINCIPLE.

There are no variables.
LOCATION.

unknown

no exact
time match
between what one is focused on
(necessarily)
and its surfacing
has a Time Lag—
on Delayed Entry.

This awareness of increased mass, or focus, blocking out all other terms, so that only the one (Focus) remains as guide and steerer of the course.

Holding tight to that, the Little Dot did arrive at the appointed spot
From whence the call originated?
Yes.
Lifting off from the physical experience of love,
NO!
YES!
that Earth scene
re-placed

Beckoned—was it?—by a "dense dot of pure energy"?
"incredibly energetic light
[to be] transformed into matter"
Her potential
if I followed
Time Zero at the end of its countdown up there overhead
the physical experience in the bedroom
missed—*more or less*?
I'd say more

the physical experience subsumed under the trip to—? who knows where?
I never found out
The scene in the bedroom unperturbed on its level
But somewhere another level took over, re-
placed it

—yet having it both ways
enveloped in sensation, the body felt all the aftermath of its devir-
gination

But what had happened in the other realm,

a spirit group gathered round
the bed

I kept mentioning them

Aloud?
Yes

Awkward, then?
Yes

As the de-virginator, boyfriend,
Listened

On the particle level
The experience
retained—Love
lifted the physical attraction to
ITS SOURCE.
      Thus, the words "I am the Alpha and the Omega" mean the
stepping-out moment, when from behind all the other experiences and
intentions and sideLIGHTS, this is the only one, the one that remains;
that everything is given for, and that then can complete its structure.*

---

*It can be on any subject, whatever one finds that is one's very own, to answer.
That perhaps no one else cares about, but that only oneself can answer—however
many jumped forms and parachutings out of the present body it could take to do
so. Could, we say. In fact, most of the parachutings take place in the particle world,
in any case, where the reason is extremely moot and has to be magnified millions
of times, to even be seen or count a jot whatsoever in this world, that is. In the particle world, perhaps it is consecutively known, for the consciousness must reside
somewhere; and they say—the particles—*there he goes again, or there she goes again,
trying to make the jump.*

    We think it a big thing, trying to make a jump from one thought to the next,
one move. But imagine a particle trying to jump from one world, the particle
one, to this one. Imagine this attempt at shift of consciousness—that is, as it
tries to get our world to deal with something on its mind. That is, on the particles's mind, which is of course your mind or my mind. Or someone's, until it
finds "that someone."

Alpha joins Omega, and it is the Living Christ presence one encounters.* Sometimes even holds, to the point of realizing that it is the Structurer. If this happens, perhaps one who also has this structure can for a moment talk to it on that level. Then lovers from the past reencounter each other, perhaps for a moment, a moment when their cellular memories are struck, electrified, touch.**

---

* This was the term I used. Terms are such difficult things. So problematical. So CONTROVERSIAL. I don't want controversy on this. Any structure will get to this position. Say, LIGHT. Pure light. "God," Creator, Maker, Allah. Well, it doesn't matter. I will accept your vocabulary, within limits.

** It now becomes clear why some theories are introduced correctly, erased into oblivion, then over centuries WORKED BACK UP TO. Right, all the time. Heavily tested. But this is—if applying, setting it down into, the law of the Alpha–Omega—allowing the whole form of it to enter backwards, forwards, upside-down, in fractions, in overstatements. All the time letting it one day precisely sit down into the Q/A formula. The quest, the answer. The search. The end-of-search.

At which point, it is considered correct, because the two hypotheticals (A/O) have been found. Both considered acceptable, at the same time. So it is a unit. It can be wielded in action. It, as a racehorse, can go out to graze. We understand it. We give it value, THROUGHOUT TIME.

But supposing it entered, stated itself correctly, way ahead of time; it was considered premature, and not different from the other hypotheticals standing beside it. How pick it out of the lineup? How know that this one was an Alpha–Omega? *That* one, merely a theory? This one, consummate and in every way mature. That one, a mere baby. Untried. Untested. Well, nevertheless, even if we weren't sure, we made sure it was WRITTEN DOWN. We put it into our hypotheticals, though unsure which side it came down on. TRUE OR FALSE. So that's how we had dealt with questions, in the past—not realizing how their wholeness *might need time, if they were entirely the thing sought for.*

But missing the intensity of the search, the baited-breath aspect, *that only centuries could supply* IN FULL EARNEST *of the type that changed the consciousness weathervane for the whole planet.* That was just the way we tested truth. Till finding out more about these variables that came with it. Accompanied. Walked in a procession with it. That took time, to understand.

IIL

*rbC

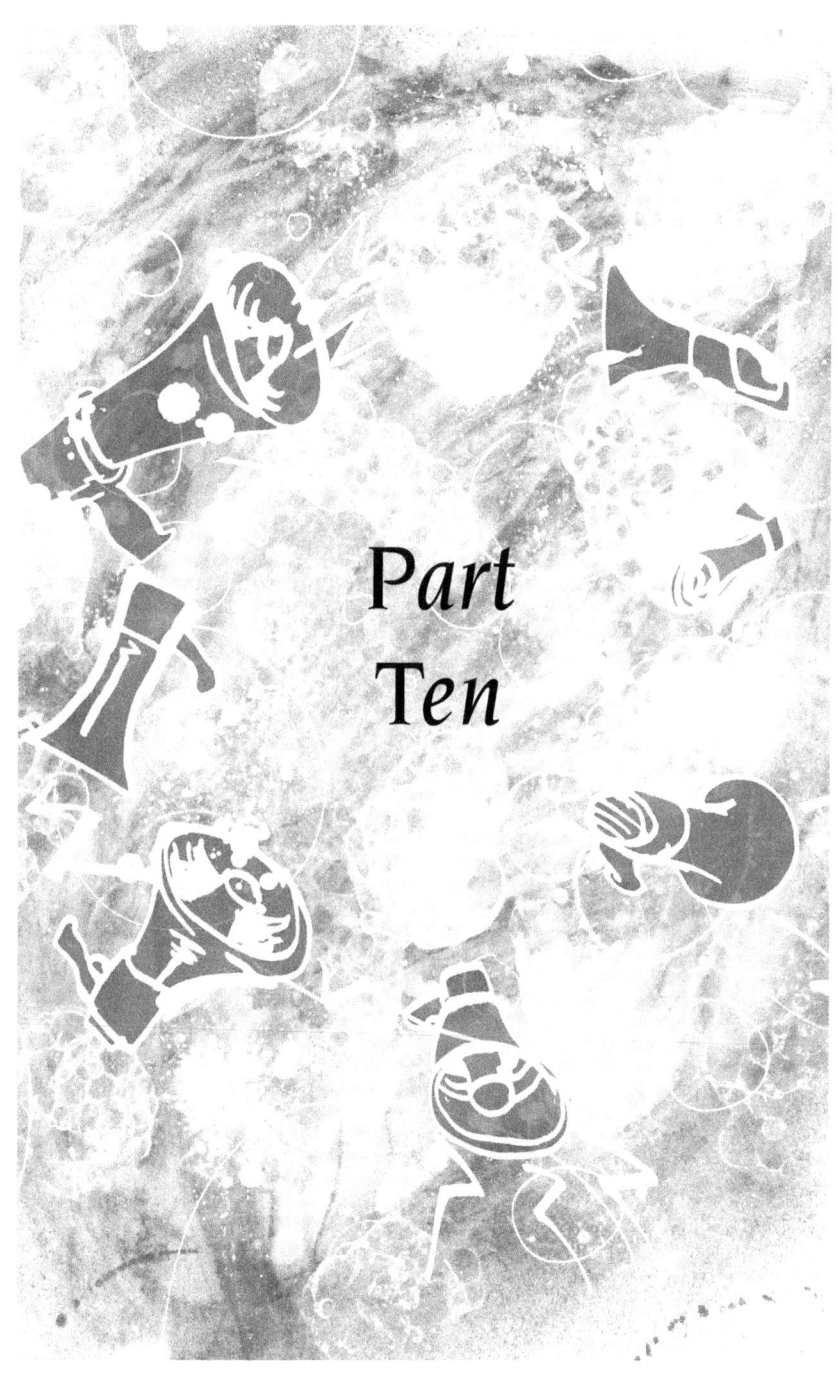

Part
Ten

Chapter Thirteen

"A Narrow Slice of

the

Electromagnetic Spectrum"—

THE OPTICAL REALM

Whereas traditional telescopes studied a
narrow slice of the electromagnetic spectrum—
the optical spectrum, which we
perceive with our eyes—radio astronomy
began the opening of the rest of the spectrum,
such as the radio, microwave, infrared,
and (in time) gamma ray frequencies. As a
result astronomers have discovered weird,
incredibly energetic phenomena.

—George Smoot, *Wrinkles in Time*

"We see what v

ve can see."

So Jesus was never real to himself except where the Christ energy was predominant. Going beyond the explanation where certain energies were included. The picture was subtler. Before reaching that point, the explanation did not count, was incomplete. Was not—and this was definitive—Alpha. Nor was it Omega. The intention was diffused, unclear, even INVISIBLE.*

---

* Suppose he wanted to communicate on a different frequency. Well, isn't that what we are saying, here?

Reality would depend on the mind, to a large extent. On "belief systems"

But this is in no way frightening.

> For me, the "final causes" of things and events are a mystery that perhaps only God knows. The scientist's job is to investigate only those causes that are prior to effects and not to speculate on occult powers of ultimate purposes.
>
> —Descartes

For any context, Descartes said you must start from and include what is "clear." That larger measures can break down, to explain smaller ones.[17] Now here the Einstein implication that the whole MUST BE greater than the sum of its parts seems violated. IS IT?

We know that the very premises against which and into which Descartes set his world model had NOTHING TO DO with the premises today. Virtually none.

Where he started—where books held knowledge, to be reflected on—is not where we start. BECAUSE *he said we shouldn't. We should start from "scratch." Erase, and then begin.*

But hold on here. We do GET KNOWLEDGE FROM scraping through earlier theories. We do set down deductions, on top of bodies of knowledge already there.

WE ARE NOT DES-CARTESIAN. Perhaps Cartesian. But we left out his entire WORLD VIEW. Is that kosher?

By Descartes own requisites. No.

What we are sure of, in the first place, was that—in some most vital way—Descartes was not cartesian. How could he be? He said THINK FOR YOURSELF.

Of the selectivity applied to what he taught, this was perhaps the most difficult and the most general. The most applicable to "the man in the street." But no one told the "woman in the street," or man there, *that thinking for oneself was* DES-CARTESIAN. They were told that larger things could be broken down into smaller and explained that way. Well, can't they? If we go back to some other lost features of that era. Such as "correspondences," "pattern linkages."

We just didn't take the leap yet, to circle up and scoop up ALL that floating in the idea "ethers" then AT THAT TIME. And therefore, what cohesion they had, TO US NOW, knowing the new principles we do.

THIS DESCARTES, let's apply THIS ONE, the one looking for unity. Let's take him at his word. And not ours. Although we had the right to make him ours. To break his mind down, his spirit, into the pieces that we could ADD UP. But wait a minute here. He said some things were "out of bounds." Off limits. HE DID. Not the way it was told to us. Some of us. Just by hearsay. As so many received what he said. Or likewise, words of the majority of our great teachers. In a time warp, WHERE they said what was appropriate FOR THEN. And no one added the remark that living thought has to be nurtured. It gets out of date. Not inherently. BUT because we think it—LIKE THE REST OF THINGS—is concrete. THUS frozen. Thought once, going once. Forever buried in a particular year. We write it on tombstones. Year of death. But what about the spirit of it???? And so genetics began to come in and teach us something

ABOUT INHERITANCE.

But starting at racing speed, we will miss some of the reasons we set out to write this—the things we wanted to EXPLORE— unless slowing with a set agenda of stops on this "visit." Visit it is, to the world here on this planet, in this universe, at this period. Visit RIGHT NOW. Visit in the contexts of THE ENTIRE UNIVERSE as a backdrop. For so much as the Earth has a history, the universe has a location behind it. Participation. More of this as we pass where it has significance.

THE SECOND COMING. We thought it would be a "real" com-ing. That an individual human being would "walk in."

Pause.* That is, many thought this. I never did.

---

* Do you mean this is our subject?

Indeed, and exactly.

It belongs to everyone, doesn't it? If it is going into Cosmic Mode.

With wildfires racing through us, on the thought level, yes it did in-deed seem time to go into this statement.

Unless one knows the experience of the highest call of one's lifetime, one cannot be experiencing any experience in the absolute sense or the sense that one might not have to one day perhaps give it up, find it used up, in this very life span.

To the extent that St. Paul was always close to this lifetime, it was governed tightly by this intention and theme: that of the Inner Christ, the Human Christ. The restatements, rejuxtapositions, the weaving of threads less clear and bright, in the combinations the message had met with. That is, diversions away from his context and most precise distinct wordings.

IN PARTICULAR, the concept of experiencing things ONCE, being COMPLETELY SURE, able to return to the premise—reenter the experience and find it always there, just as it was THE FIRST TIME (in a sense, the only time when it had been this much of a surprise)—had been completely lost in the "shuffle," in relation to the evolutions of the centuries since. The increasing need to find answers outside, to even make one's truth match what was "expected" and pronounced, by common verdict, the truth, was ever moving away from his philosophy. Similarly, the grand encounter of Descartes with the truth, his wiping everything from his mind—every assumption—to put there only what passed the test of certitude (that one could return to and find unchanged), was the test of St. Paul. This unwavering certainty, this Lack of Change (opposite from "this universe of change"), had also been signaled out BY PLATO.

This necessity for OUTER replication—as if *if all the world believed, one might become certain oneself, or that if all the world believed, they would* MAKE IT TRUE by sheer force of mass focused on that truth—was not where Descartes had "found his truth;" nor was it the method he advocated. Nor did Einstein, when disbelieving the implications that might be drawn from his theory, turn toward the outer Descartes, the tradition-established methodical Descartes. He turned toward the genius Descartes, the original Descartes, the one he was resembling in this feature.

Chunking Down the 21st Century Gestalt:
The Earth in the evolutionary position
of moving from lower to higher mind: of changing its relative
consciousness. Joining the Species of LIFE:
To Join With
Or

Not?[*]

---

[*] Throwing it down, from out there in space. Picturing it like that. As if chunks of new energy were falling to the ground.

As to Newton, what about his statement, in *Mathematical Principles*, Book III, that "The most beautiful System of the Sun, Planets and Comets could only proceed from the counsel and dominion of an intelligent and powerful being"? Where's the proof? Where's the plan? He racked his brain. Did experiments. Practiced alchemy. And couldn't find it.

Not knowing about germs, he did not know that the very predicament—or situation—he was in, the map of the gestalt, offered a clue. Did not see that the tiny physical germ (on the rat, transporting the flea) was causing death—not just of people but of the mentality, in lieu of the one that would prevail in the centuries ahead.But what (he did not ask) could it possibly have to do with the fact that he was on *alternate current, as it were*? His mind was spinning, intensifying, catching fire, understanding things, putting them together—functioning as a whole—while all of London (from which he had escaped, retreated) was being attacked (many killed). Why the reverse? Had it to do with two orders of reality, where the idea itself was the very living substance of protection or healing; in its very intention and context, it was the very destiny of the idea that somehow caused him to survive, as he "carried" the idea. But what a thought. WHAT COULD IT POSSIBLY MEAN???

It is like saying that Newton's "destiny" protected him, IN THE SENSE THAT THE IDEA HAD TO SURVIVE. It was *in the future. How was it going to get there? if not through a human "carrier"?? Or was the future indeterminate? Here complexity combines with multiply scaled ladderlike content,* where a single thing can be multiply leveled at the same time, and the general visible physical EFFECT or situation can even appear negative, to the collective—when something in it is dying, as it were.

Such as an age's mentality, for instance. Similarly, to this, there was a slaughter at the Birth of Christ. A new idea was coming in. NEW ENERGY WAS. In reality, something on a greater scale was dying. Throughout history in the future, the picture would continue to be held up. The geography of birth, accompanied by slaughter of the innocents, had entered the human trajectory as the birth of a new idea. That part is now being CORRECTED.

Davies, ibid. (page 271):

> "Can we believe that the universe is not only bio-friendly but mind-friendly too?"

Quoting Stephen Jay Gould in *Life's Grandeur* (1996), as cited in *The Fifth Miracle* (Paul Davies, page 272): "If the evolutionary drama were to be rerun [due to all life on Earth being wiped out but microbes], what would happen? Would we expect a broadly similar pattern of development, with fish, vertebrates, reptiles, mammals, and intelligent bipeds re-emerging? Not a bit of it, he [that is, Gould] concludes."

Well, we explore. We reserve judgment. In illustration, Davies writes, page 266: "A good example of biological regress is Spiegelman's monster that I discussed in chapter 5. There the spoon-fed RNA slimmed itself down to a fraction of its original viral size in order to replicate faster"; i.e., have no "excess baggage." If spoon-fed, it laid aside all redundancies. No organs that it no longer needed. Fortunately, we are not spoon-fed. ALTHOUGH some proponents of information usages see that as the goal. To spread it, make it totally available, lay it out on the table, all for one, one for all—leaving scope, work, and comprehension to those that care to work out the unnecessary details.

266: "A good exa
discussed in chapt
fraction of its origin
baggage." This was
organs that it n
ALTHOUGH son
spread it, make i
all—leaving scope,
to work out the un
OK. That
the visible and the

OK. That's how I became interested in this concept of the double level: the visible and the invisible. The apparent. And the Below Comprehension. To not leave out
the *apparently redundant*, to go back even and pick those things up—those things too far ahead to be seen as instruments too, for the growth of our civilization if it thought in terms of a very long future.

So Davies has shown me that the areas of question gone into in his book, if taken back through Goethe and Darwin, connected as they already are, then up to Jung, then to the concept sounded into my head at the piano, the ritual—playing right through to the end of the pre-written piece—that that would do it.

That this too, like the dream of the child Jung, was one of humanity's dreams, that happened to be filtered through this brain, AS OTHER CONCEPTS WERE FILTERED ELSEWHERE. But with everything interactive, as it was, it meant that every single brain has some CONNECTION to this idea. Readers, then come. Access these ideas far deep inside you. Come read, sit with me. Let us review what the Universe has left for us to use. Find that place inside where this all makes sense to you, no matter when, no matter where.

And Various and Sundry Pages This Led to

So it appears that two ideas of the Whole were active at the same time. While, in Newton's time, one—the individually dispersed masses—held the old, the other (the One but in the human, condensed container) contained for the Whole its *future mentality. Now, this is too important for us to ignore (or be "ignorant of," any longer). The heir apparent—the future controlling idea—as pushed up from the past and attracted into and from (?) the future, as simply the "jump" out of the straight line, of the masses through the straight line of the "emerging" spirit of the times,* could not be so intensified, if spread out in numbers. It **defied quantifying numbers,** unified the old into a single point (of the new); in so doing, so organized itself that those left behind and dragging their feet and on another brain-wave entirely, as before a force of nature, but it was a force of—or Above—mind, went down under it! As before the movement of time, of a raging river. Of the unincorporated, unrelenting, unfinished, some-times called unredeemed, energies—even entities—that did not find a way to end their energies when their lives, in the human defi-nition, ended. All this, part of the human condition, in life as well as before/after. All this, inside the Now of Life, as it chose itself, in the way our tendencies have partly directed and shaped it—what it has to expend with, delete, to keep the species, itself, going. And it cannot speak what it does if there is no "hearing." If communication has not reached this far. On the other hand, this faculty of ability to "hear" that Newton had, was directed toward what reality on Earth was, due to the facts of its past and future, but not to control that he had over what might accompany the situation in events. **The mighty shifting of the currents, of what was "*known*" in reality on the Earth, in the minds of the majorities, did mean that to take away the realities of their minds, at this point in time, required a giant shift. And this came through the ideas the brain could comprehend. It did not come up through the backbone,** as we in the West had dispensed with intelligence that might be acquired through that.

Of what use were our brains if we had high-speed, supersonic technology, at least going in that direction? We developed mentally through the brain. The physical eyesight, accompanied by perception, which it depended on, mostly. The nervous system could not handle too-great shocks and voltages of electricity, or even of mind-view. So it could not move, organically, such energy. It stumbled, "started," jolted forward again—under the weight. It had to be funneled through the brain. The brain, that up to this point, worked in verbal "idea" structures. SO FAR AS IT KNEW. AND FOR THE MOST PART. It knew flashes—but in the brain, sometimes the visual brain. It did not know the movement up the spinal column. Not in general. So long as the masses could not sense information to any great degree—not sniff it out in the air, for instance—many did in fact rely on intelligence of guesswork (practical feet-on-the-ground that happened to have wisdom in it, foresight). But the movement upward through the spinal cord into insight, this remained for the future. For the large part.

So we are enquiring whether there was a parallel between the large numbers (the quantitative humanity) and the One, which—apparently—introduced its Start, its Big Bang, of a new idea in a CONCERTED EFFORT. Unleashed itself, through a Goliath paradigm. It sought out Newton's mind. The fleas took the rest, the populace, the old, in hand. That was it. It was CHECKMATE FOR THE POPULACE, as the "single-minded" new outdid the "divided old." As the slaughter of the "innocents" replayed. Not named that (i.e., in the seventeenth century). For there was no detected culprit. Except of course germs, when discovered—the rat, the flea. How blame them? They were certainly NO CAESAR. Not one single historian raised the idea, the banner, that "history was repeating itself," with a view to the first century AD. With regard to an archetype related to CHANGE. And what then, now, as a double millennium tries to

assert,

with authority,

WHICH is its master; i.e., what involvements—what consciousness—will "reign"? Who will it crown? What will be its star
achievements? Unspyed out, it has come in, like always, in the
concertedness of a single focus. Even if using a group, to create
and compact "the single." Or several groups, with this large a world
population. But it would separate, like always. That is, then, how
the PIANO PIECE ENDED. A concert. A concerted FOCUS. But what

does that mean? Is it that the new, the Alpha–Omega, was always complete when it first got sight of itself? We broke it up. And then, so as to understand the concept "unity of FIELD," we would ANSWER A QUESTION

WE HAD LONG PUT TO OURSELVES.

What we have observed is the *parallel unity of field of the withdrawn, secluded Newton*, whose "prismatic intelligence" was receiving the restructuring, the eureka!, of the old (brought to resolution) EVEN AS the old itself, unresolved, was—qualitatively, in the numbers of locations of its thought processes (human beings, as a matter of fact)—soundly exterminated.

By the rats, that were carrying the fleas, that were carrying the Black Death. The Black Plague. It is phenomenal. *How there was so much (none of which we knew, therefore saw) revealed in this little package.*

A package of insight, was it? Not in sight to us. Not yet, no. Well, not in sight for centuries, this bargain between the collective and "the one," stealing through the battlefield, carrying off the packet the masses would need. Those that did not die in the collective slaughter. But we are talking about the future—those masses—the direction of the world. The course it would take, guided by this packet—that "escaped." Newton riding on horseback as in the midnight ride of Paul Revere to alert the troops the British were coming. Not the Brits, of course, here, but danger in the form of fleas carrying the deadly disease that was wiping out whole cities, almost. With no defense, no antibiotics, no vaccinations, no information even. No, they "did not know."

Shall we call it a little quantum of pattern, of the very explication of the concept? For he was the **unified field** *representative—in the line of The Big* "TOE." The designated "One." Which the All temporarily entered, in a manner of speaking. To set forth our next field. Though he was single, we would be numerous. The unified field, contrasted (in the one place) by the scattered nonunified field (or rather, it too was unified, but by death), invisibly in the nontheory of germs and disease. So the nontheory, from which our modern genetics is a descendant and branch, has NEVER BEEN TRACED BACK TO HERE. Standing in parallel to Newton himself, whom it did not kill. But that would probably require knowing something about inheritance. (No, not yet. Not yet). Of course, we skipped all that for a while back then. Opening up the subject of germs (which the newly invented microscope allowed), which had remained closed, then, we enter the age NOT ENTERED THEN. Leaving the age that Newton brought in. Is it not a careful balance—that he did not look there, when he was spared (unaffected), by the *disease causes* that were being demonstrated? He looked to planetary motion, weights, force, attraction. ETC. But what of what he did not look to. There, we look at present.

How economical—of Nature, of Consciousness—that it yields forth for us, in the light of modern understanding, the very seeds it LIKEWISE PLANTED, by demonstrating *then* in the Event World; or let us call it, as it has been labeled, Event FIELD. The event field of the 1700s—of what we DID NOT integrate then— Why, it hung around. It's ready now. We can *see* it, now—when now we so need it. To counteract the discoveries of Newton. As *he himself would be the first to agree*. We did not exactly hold out to him the alchemy he so searched for. At any rate, this would intrigue him. To counteract our counteraction of some of the energy laws he put together. For now that we see further than he did, into the quantum, nature DEMANDS THAT we understand *the field that century was in*. The entire field. The unity. The two sides. The opposites. The newborn idea and the dying/giving-birth idea. And the concealed *later seeds*. The pod, in fact, the seed cluster. And not just the one developed in the centuries ahead. But the womb it came from. The entire unity of the mentality, still growing, that creates—now and into the future—the consciousness we live in. Each and every one. IN OUR MINDS. Seeping into every event we all share. And this will not be MECHANICAL. This explanation. Having allowed "mechanics" sway for several centuries, we have seen demonstrated HOW TO AVOID AND ANSWER IN ADVANCE ARGUMENTS GOING IN THAT DIRECTION. We take the Einsteinian compass. We head DOWN THE MIDDLE. Mainstream. That will do it.

We should not forget the BIG T

OW

    hush, no more said, undesignated, unspecified, line
    of des
    CARTE, for
    instance? that we associated with a Big Tow, an ARTISTS' TOW,
down though HisTO-
Ry
back to Latin
the lineage of
OE

Afterword

I can see a being who stands on the top of mountains, calling out to the elements. They come. I can see this as it happened. Was it in the past? Where? But there is no hourglass here. I see it, in my mind's eye. Again? No, it is the first time. The new consciousness began its arriving.

Everything was different in it. It was like the first step into the Hita nadi, where the photography used the light of the sun. Like the spread of that, so quickly, bringing unknown images and answers. As if the shapes of time and the instruments in it—the shapes of the elements, even—were seen more abstractly. It was a new universe. An old one. It was a real Prospero beginning. Commanding the elements, bringing them close, talking to them and telling them, like Father Time, what was in store; and did they want to be part of it? And what then? They discussed and drew lots, perhaps. Then put on their costumes. Only one way of seeing it. Behind the stories were the archetypes rumbling and roaring and mixing together, such as how Charlotte Brontë became despondent despite the success of her novel *Jane Eyre*—published, under a male name, Currer Bell, in October, just before her sister Emily was booed out of life. Triumph in art coming in temporal parallel to her sister dying in despair and nontriumph, outright rejection—albeit officially it was tuberculosis that got her.

Just as if the two sisters, two books, *Jane Eyre* and *Wuthering Heights*, published almost the same month, were a pair of particles that one being appreciated, the other was scorned—the public not ready for Ellis Bell. Well, if we had any doubt about this hypothesis, look at the scientific name under which *paired opposite-spin particles* were first described: Bell's Theorem.

No!

And to bring me a little bit in, recall the subtle (nonphysical) *bell* that came into my apartment in 1991 at the start of these writings. I didn't bring the bell into this book, but you can read about it in most of my others.

So, is it possible the Bell Theorem and the Bell sisters (who took the name out of their far-seeing poetic imaginations) have *absolutely nothing in common*, though they describe the same thing? Paired particles and nonlocal causality?

But *that's not proof.*

If you say so.

A splashy "coincidence" slapping you in the face—nothing to see there.

What about my bell being such a large a part of my spiritual initiations?

Another coincidence.

I really can't wrap my head about it.

And what about Abelard and Héloise (silent 'h")?

No? Yes?

Back to the story.

And this went on, into the time streams of humanity—THAT LESSON. THERE WERE UNCOUNTABLE EXAMPLES MORE. So now, the Old Man said, let us close this installment in our past. Let us look for the next lessons, even still with us, in the WAITING LIST. There are so many active, storm-tossed arrivals, newly in town from the ship, just for a night out. All these lessons could descend at any moment on anyone. And each one carries with it the same conclusion: TO CHANGE THE END.

On the verge of waking, I dreamed of a man sitting at a table, where his book had just been put onto TV; an advertisement, I think. It showed figures *between* human figures. Animated, as parts of the person left out, invisible, in normal vision. VISIBLE ON THE SCREEN. In between matter.

Enrapturing.

It dramatized, animatedly, individual dynamics. There was also a photo, or background image, as of an atomic bomb. Only, larger, if possible—or in the mind of someone surprised to find it so near. Yet to this he seemed to pay no attention.

It rose to the sky.

His message in the last year had gone to every corner of the Earth.

I wanted to speak to him; he modestly said, "I'm the host here."

I woke. THE HOST. The author of the information. It was the "host's" information. Then I thought: *What could it mean, to think of humans as having a Host? and humanity having an Unconscious Host? Being an unconscious host? The host of immortality,*[*]

---

[*] I cannot say to what emotional lengths this image drove me, how it held out—as with a carrot on a stick—something in the future.

Of course, this was—in 1998—long before the image of the towering cloud of fiery smoke, on 9/11, 2001. He was interested in what happened in between events (and people, in hard, sure outlines). In between, the real motives, connectors, communications, lay.

in fact.

I thought of the face of the ancient Teacher on the wall in the cave in Romania. There was more to that I thought I would learn, as well. Perhaps he was the man in the dream, and in some universe it was already known, even, as his book. Well, how can we know?

✳

The consecrated wafer and wine of the Eucharist. Ah-ha, a pun? Signaling presence, as in the "host" of the sacrament?

My mind jumps to the scrap of bread the two beggars fought over, tearing it apart—a demolition derby—in Baudelaire's poem "Le Gâteau," that later somehow, in a hop and a skip, connected, in me (unconsciously, of course) at Le Dôme Café in Paris, France, at the sight of the miming beggar at my window—the returning Ulysses?—signaling electrically? Making me sit bolt upright at the café table to begin my series. Well, the fragmented scraps of *le pain* led the poet to ask: where was the place where bread was cake? Nonlocal, no doubt.

Elijah "looked, and, behold, there was a cake baked on the coals" just before ravens fed him, till after there was no more to drink, because the brook dried up, he was told by the Lord to go into a town, where a widow there would take over—giving him, with water, bread, "cakes" of it. In the Elijah paradigm the handful of meal and trace of oil supplied nonstop food.

And was that what I picked up indirectly, in 1965, as a theme activating in me this series, of (untitled then) *Love in Transition: Voyage of Ulysses: Letters to Penelope*?

As the explosion rose as high as an atomic bomb in the dream, and there was no dust to settle because there was no dust, we will fervently hope that part was figurative.

The atmosphere in the dream was positive. That seemed to mean there was energy enough to overthrow the background warning. Not let that future get much further. That he, and not it, was the Host here, of the decisions.

Fear was not the ruler, not the dominator. And was he also saying NOT TO PAY ATTENTION TO the negative situation, right there backing him, though not backing him up in any sense of the term, for he had a book that emphasized THE POSITIVE and that around the globe it was being read (but how?); anyway, which was stronger, that cloud of smoke over there, or He, THE HOST???????? Was he, in fact, in between the events, in a way, his energy the interstitcher, if he was in fact the HOST????

Was it, in fact, to the Earth??? And certainly a Host knew how to keep his guests safe!!

—the connections, the energies, the invisible FORCES that were the place where—in between the physical—a subtle energy had influence. In fact, *the decisive vote*. He was there, sending out his writing vibrations (at least as the dream showed it) to people who in fact, he said, PICKED THEM UP. All over the world, read the words of (the vibrations of) himself, THE HOST. He was here, speaking, and out there, they were bombing, as if he were not here. Yet he was the "host," and the real power, the ability to avert such things, lay IN BETWEEN THE ACTUALITIES OF WHAT WAS VISIBLE. Working in where the real power lay.

Figuratively, the rat is the host of the flea, or the plant is the host of pollen. So what did it mean here, if we deciphered the statement? Did that have to do with the focus on the IN-BETWEEN!! The energy, the interactions, the connections, the (for now) unconscious energetics??!! This was the focus of the Host's book, which had circled the globe. WHAT DID THAT MEAN???

By 2002 the answer came in a most emphatic way. I went to an intuitive (highly trained) chiropractor, who worked in touching trigger points (with Light).

The Kundalini began to bubble, to fizz, to ignite, seemingly cell to cell—passing through new openings. All throughout my body, there was rejoicing, I felt, as if a pole of Light was sitting there, holding the ecstaticness of a collective energy somewhere, racing up and down in cosmic rejoicing and even orgasm as one cell, touching the other, opened it with the emotion. This was the reignition of these words, the re-visioning of them inside the body.

The very next day I woke to walk, as in a trance, to this part of the book series and sit and relate that cellular ignition and transmission to this point of the Earth. I quickly add that such a situation has no local limitation if it does not want to. IT CAN SELF-REPLICATE if it wants to. It already probably existed elsewhere! But it walked inside me. It brought the column of Light. And what did the cellular response contain? The sensation, to me, of cosmic ecstasy, on a plane anybody can go to, in direction, a focus, anybody can move the attention to, suppose this kind of energy moved into them. And why not? A wish for the Earth, the Host said. He is moving this energy in between all the events of the Earth, interstitching it WITH THIS JOY AND LOVE. passing it like a ball of wildfire, back and forth and everywhere, as the Earth ASCENDS.

For I knew, in my mind, it was Ascension energy. I believe it was the feeling of Ascension, as in the Transfiguration and Ascension of the Christ story on Earth. That Ascension, experienced in the One, can—just as in Newton's story recounted here—enter the masses as a new Consciousness. It can become the experience of the Earth, and Mother Earth, passed down in the human cellular layers, just as it also passes through the atmospheres around events, the interstices, letting them know in some dimension their location IN THE HOST.

Watching and seeing in her own mind's eye, assisting, sending Light through her fingers, the chiropractor said, "There is more Light than fear on the Earth." Just like in the dream: "I'm the Host here."

I started out on my own stay-at-home voyage, as, figuratively, Penelope. Fittingly. Half my name comes from my grandmothers— true story—Margaret Penelope.

Milton had said—and I bring back out—

"We belong on Mount Parnassus together
We both have an appetite for dew"

Wait a minute. Other players get to speak up.

What about
—an unknown theme level and thread through time
Parnassus *Street*?
Did that count?
Hunter Thompson writing to me from?
his home on?
Parnassus
Street

"Somewhere there must be a place where bread is cake." A-hem

No, le-hem

Is it a crossword puzzle? What's the answer?

In Hebrew, Beth = "house"

and "bread"? (*Lehem.*)

Gingerbread? That's it. That's the spirit. Bread House.

�֍

So it must have been (I said to myself) that this whole past year, 2023, of not being able to get (necessary to me) energy from a computer-printout interaction (which did not follow me to America when I left Europe way back in 2001; no, as I pressed "type," what came out was exactly what was on-screen, and the accompanying peaks of excitement had receded too) that silence, stillness, was to was to get me to bring out what had already been incubated, in some cases drafted.

And after I picked back up those drafts, something else came to delight me: tangible, visible energy floating—yes, visible, in sparkles—at a standstill, at my side sometimes or dancing. Or making circles, glittering, around me, saying: Keep going. Intervening to cheer me on, saying: Look who's here!!!!!!!!

They just appeared right now, on my right, blocking a tip end of what I am writing from view, these energy beings . . . now not so much a wave or a dazzling point collection. Instead with—triangle shapes? I cannot totally make it out. *Here—surprise, surprise.* Then they grew stronger; they occupied the left Field of my vision. Kept near me. Like a floating brigade, a magic carpet, a contingent, of travelers, in a group, a platoon, a battalion, a mission of airplanes, strange shaped, ET to be sure? Well, what else? Their purpose?

For now, they remind me they are with me. They exist. How deny it? Oh, sure. Reason says to. But what is this book about? Taking the measure of life through your own experience. Goethe, Leonardo, all of you perhaps as such flying light beings now, traveling in that fashion, planting ideas, dropping them, spraying them, just emitting them as you pass by, pass along. Many more where they came from. No pride of ownership. No?

Tremendous pride of ownership.

Hurry back soon. A hint. At the right side of the computer table. Bon Voyage.

Becoming distant as only a few remain. At the crown now. Points of consciousness? Still hinting.

If your light blurs my vision, that's OK
Physically, that is,
You open screen porches,
Rip the wire enclosing them
Open the daylight to deeper daylight
To where your Light is fluttering and deeply waving to me
From
While
Right
Here
Visibly

Objectively
I'll swear to it
You are
Objectively
HERE
This minute

I must insert—still under the sensations, the memories, of how the cells felt yesterday—that this must be one expression of working "in between events"—including where the cells (inside us, just like the quantum forces, the atomic energy, the electricity, is inside us)—that this entire capability of the Earth, which had so far experienced it technologically, was granted (as had been the hope, the natural outcome, all the time) to US CITIZENS. Not only a mechanical development, but the subtle, the HUMAN.

Yes, I felt taken into custody, under the wing, in some way ("you are," I hear) that was precisely wise and right. Naturally, of course, it portended well for the whole globe if this much intercession was confidently taking place. And I report on this one spot. This much choice offered the Earth in 180-degree opposition—love and fear (the energies therewith)! Offered privately "between the stitches." Of Penelope's handiwork? Well, in part.

Fear was also throwing out all the Stops, acting like a candle, and that came from the TOW.

Pardon, you write it TOE.

The what? The Theory of Everything?

If you say so.

The waving dimension of Light is gone now.

Quick, gone in an eyeblink, though it stayed long for that dimension, in human time, considering the lifetime of a particle. Were photons joining in, dying. replaced instantly in our reckoning, faster in theirs, "new" particles being created to, right off, be part of the exhibition, the only experience they would have in their short-to-us life? Born for that "purpose'? That "end"?

Charles Darwin: From *The Descent of Man*, Chapter 21 (1871) Excerpt, pages 1608–1613: *The Norton Anthology of English Literature*, 5th edition, vol. 2, M. H. Abrams, General Editor. New York: W. W. Norton & Co. 1962/1986.

Clarifying *The Origin of Species*, page 1609:

The main conclusion arrived at in this work, and now held by many naturalists who are well competent to form a sound judgment, is that man is descended from some less highly organized form. The grounds upon which this conclusion rests will never be shaken, for the close similarity between man and the lower animals in embryonic development, as well as in innumerable points of structure and constitution, both of high and of the most trifling importance—the rudiments which he retains, and the abnormal reversions to which he is occasionally liable—are facts which cannot be disputed. They have long been known, but until recently they told us nothing with respect to the origin of man . . . He who is not content to look, like a savage at the phenomena of nature as disconnected cannot any longer believe that man is the work of a separate act of creation. He will be forced to admit that the close resemblance of the embryo of man to that, for instance, of a dog—the construction of his skull, limbs, and whole frame, independently of the uses to which the parts may be put, on the same plan with that of other mammals—the occasional reappearance of various structures, for instance of several distinct muscles, which man does not normally possess, but which are common to the Quadrumana—and a crowd of analogous facts—all point in the plainest manner to the conclusion that man is the codescendant with other mammals of a common progenitor.

Profoundly repulsed by his view of what he termed "barbarian," he stated (page 1612): "For my own part I would as soon be descended from that heroic little monkey, who braved his dreaded enemy in order to save the life of his keeper; or from that old baboon, who, descending from the mountains, carried away in triumph his young comrade from a crowd of astonished dogs—as from a savage who delights to torture his enemies, offers up bloody sacrifices, practices infanticide without remorse, treats his wives like slaves, knows no decency, and is haunted by the grossest superstitions." So wrote Darwin, 1871, referring to his experiences in the South Seas on HMS Beagle in 1832 (The *Voyage of the Beagle*, Chapter 10).

He concludes—in a sentence still valid: "Having risen . . . to the very summit of the organic scale" (page 1620), with "noble qualities," "benevolence," "godlike intellect which has penetrated into the movements and constitution of the solar system—with all these exalted powers—Man still bears in his bodily frame the indelible stamp of his lowly origin" (page 1613).*

---

* But one notices that much of his value assertions and observations are related to emotional evolution, as opposed to mental. Mental faculties sharpened. But emotional evolution? This was a point that Darwin was eloquent on as he likewise returned to look backward on his main point from the study of the origin of species.

I realized—

No, I realized nothing of the sort (but we will go on as if I did; at the moment I realized nothing at all)—that the consciousness I had reached thought of itself as containing whatever (or at least a large degree of whatever, from my point of view) in the universe met it, merged with it, acted in concert with it, in unity at any moment. It could *look around into the universe (itself), for what it wanted to explore next,* what solution had already been reached, what there was to bring together, to do. That the universe was expanding meant there was also further to go. That hanging on to its coattails meant there was always something exciting, something new. Worthwhile, no doubt. To know. To do.

✳

Pages and pages back, we found advice from some of our greatest geniuses, Leonardo and Goethe, which said *look inside*. Simply put, they practiced "self-study." They valued experience: observation in nature, not—or, in Goethe's case, not only—an indoor laboratory setting. With almost no technology in Leonardo's day, no one thought of such a disconnection: to let laboratories (cut off from nature) and machines, doubly, triply cut off, not knowing firsthand what nature was, be The Observers. It's *cock-eyed*, he would have said. *It defies my common sense, however uncommon*. Invent "the scientific method"? No. Not his cup of tea. Now, take Ben Franklin, standing under a shed roof for safety in 1752, holding a string of a kite he was flying in a storm—an outdoor laboratory—as electricity lost no time in electrifying the wiry metal conductor in a Mason jar. "His observations laid the groundwork for later scientists, including Michael Faraday and Thomas Edison, to further explore the mysterious properties of electricity."[18] But Leonardo's imagination, too, his own perceiving eyes and senses, the scientific method downplays and defies.

※

> "The Upanishads say that in the region of the heart is a hollow space the size of the tip of the thumb which contains all things," wrote Dhyanyogi-ji, a saint, sage, sat guru, in the twentieth century. Reporting things he *could not know*, said the West. Self -observation was not that smart. "All elements, all things, regardless of whether they are present or absent in the immediate external environment, are present in this microscopic universe in the heart."

But how could you know about what's microscopically in the heart—without a microscope! See, got cha!

Further: "Yogis believe that life exists around millions of stars, based on the searches made up to this time."

Set in Sanskrit terminology, theirs was not the Western "ether," the one of the alchemists, of Newton. It was another entirely. Nor was it Newtonian; that is, unless one might ask if Newton knew of THIS ether. It could have respectfully entered the argument on the "content" of space (did it have matter in it or not?).

Because here, precisely, was where the Easterners had something to say. Of course, they said, space had matter in it. Einstein had agreed, but this had been the beginning of a debate as to how much. Certainly not the de Sitter model. No, even, one model said, space was all but empty, relatively. And that was that. But in the East, it emphatically was not.

If we did not peer carefully, how would we know the base, the uncut-off roots; they come with words like "sound"? We would not.

Whereas "sound," in Sanskrit, takes for granted it is not the external "sound." Not merely. BUT THE PROCESS OF CREATION OF SOUND.

It would be complex, embedded with (in the Eastern case) centuries of investigation—of self-study, if you will. But *how is it our greatest Western thinkers, artists, knew about this concept of self-study—they did it—and Western science had not heard their upraised voices, apparently. Not crediting the working technique of these greatest minds to work in finding truth in their field as they found it in universal expressions not called "science."* Lacking the word. Even, here, we might have to stretch, to shift back, from right brain to left.

Thus, the Third Eye to remind us that at birth any individual contains divine energy.

We see once again the universal symbols in Carl Jung's first dream. The Ajna (Third Eye) means "toward knowledge." To stop the movement means to stop the awareness, that did not look outward but stared forever—at what? the frozen top of its world—no involvement with motion. Freezing Light? How dare it?

Like a sailboat when the wind dies down, our consciousness, our state of knowledge, the Light anchored, in this dream image. But how is it possible? The "top" of the Earth seemingly nailed on tight. The winds of change must blow very hard, indeed. Perhaps into unwanted events, or "highly energized" events, when the intention was to broaden the vision. But that message unreceived. No. The fixed eye remained "unmoved," incapable of looking outside its fixed view: once and forever, this is how it is. But how totally boring that would be. What a safe, uninteresting Earth. Surely this idol is easy to topple. We have tried. I have.

It may take a few more centuries?????—what about a year? A week? A few more days? Or no time, instantaneous on contact—to understand *in clear, plain English*. And to align as a species with those few simple plain English words??????.

Me playing the arpeggios and runs of a Bach piece—in recital—a tiny, nervous seven-year-old. What did I know? Nothing. Not even how to finish the piece.

And suddenly—a launching pad into a time scale?? Picked up. How? Why?

Like a cartoon character.

By the Paris beggar.

Who was "mar"-
RUNED

Little did he know.
He didn't have to.
No Marvel Cinematic cameras
No film hero

The universe targeted and BEAMED IN here. Just like a reconstructed, materializing messenger.

Out of a children's book?
If you will.
The mouth—moving up and down in *wavy lines.*

What did you say?
Yes, making waves, he was.
across the window—.
Dazzling?
No, not like—
the wavy lines *that came to visit me, in this very room,*
obvious, twinkling

battalion
to my right side
just this minute

as I sat on February 24, 2024, at my computer,
about sixty—that's right—years later.

Sometimes they come, these wave beings, whose twinkling compels a
trance. I dare you not to fall into one, seeing them, if they visit.
Dancing just off to one side of me
Or you,
if there

visible to the outer eye

The one the child Jung saw frozen AND SINGULAR
Object-like

Pancakelike on the top of the "creature" enthroned
in his DREAM?
　　　　As if time were in a cryonic state?
Frozen Light?

Help! Help! Mallarmé
Chunks of meaning to weed out—

　　　　Just listen to the "connections," he pipes in

That's what got me into this mess

　　　　No, not *you* listen
　　　　Listen to the
　　　　listening imagination
　　　　that hears the sounds faster than you do
　　　　subtle connections
SOUND OFF

What are you talking about?

I want the sound on
I just called in Mallarmé

    I'm Mallarmé

    Sound off
    1, 2, 3, 4
    Clear the air
    Sound off
    Then you can hear better

    Un-
    Herd
    Sounds
    Sound off
    Clear the air
    Listen
    better

PK-experiment cage pictured in photo of parapsychologist
J. B. Rhine and me
DICE in rotating cage
—handed down through centuries
the question
what was chance?
AND WHAT NOT?

Do it—be self-aware
Goethe and Leonardo *shouting their lungs out*
Or simply *beckoning with the subtlest of miming*

Chance
playing on TV
—the popular series—
In my room
when in North Carolina my mother died
mimicking each other
one on, one off the TV screen—
two experiences attracted to me
the scene on TV visible
come to tell my emotions in Virginia what they couldn't see
what my mother, in another state
was enduring
driver smashing into the car she was riding in, her body killed
as I watched the simultaneous
replica
clairvoyant?
AN ACTIVE (Action!) SYMBOL

But on TV, Chance, a character,
intercepted the out-of-control car

not so, the other car

synchronistic pair
where—as in the cojoined/separated particles in the aforemen-

tioned
Bell theorem
the fate of one *is the opposite* of the other

Chance
Looked both ways
split

electrical linkages
up the spine
Third Eye
Yes, single
Not staring

"In non-amazement,"
Faulkner pipes in
stoniness
inflexible
inattention

to detail

"Non-amazement," Faulkner says again, capturing it for us
his self-awareness at fever pitch
his self-observation
let it never be said his was lagging or slow to catch on

eye Ulysses put out
Single, giant,

Third?
SAYING THE SAME THING!!!!!

in the moving in-between left-out bits of time, Life, events, and
FORCES
the inter-
stitches

as Penelope
W'
OVE

L'
OVE
in
TRANS-
ition

Just as if weaving a universal situation in
string
superstring
theory

Or *loop quantum gravity?*

and was she?
did Penelope do it?
time weave, woven inter-
stitches
rippling
the *time shapes and forms*
yes, we have said time carries them like balloons in the air
sewing and un-SO?
-ing
Love
'N
transition

A loaf of bread
foot
sole
PRINT
ov'
n

of the human fires of the heart in transition

"BREAD
Street London"
Baudelaire pipes up

Newton born there?
No, yes
—it's hard to confirm
an obscure fact, what with all the street names changing,

You know
Beth-
lehem
"House
of Bread"
Bread
Street? I just thought there might be a connection

Well, perhaps
Hold on, was he born on December 25

Funny that you asked
was Newton born
On?
You guessed it
December 25

On Bread Street?

to be exact
NO
but we nailed it down

Bread Street
City, 46, Cheapside (EC4) "So called, of bread in old time there sold.
. . . A side-entry or alley led from this street to the famous "Mermaid" Tavern frequented by Shakespeare, Ben Jonson, Sir Walter Raleigh, and their contemporaries).[19]

What? Shakespeare went there?
Ben Johnson?
At just a side alley away

Of course
Let it be known:

> "On the wall of Bow Bells House is a City of London blue plaque, recording that the poet and statesman John Milton was born in Bread Street in 1608."[20]

You see why Newton saw *every*thing as being connected
Without, mind you, knowing why
It just was, take it from him, he said
He being as confused about it as the next person

Though as if in evidence
Or call it moral support for his very own self,
The universe wrapped him in this swaddling puzzle
born on December 25, then
right along with it,
just, naturally,
his birthplace got entangled
why, only 2,305 miles away
Mediterranean Sea to cross
doable
BREAD Street
Dinky, rural, could be an exact replica of those Bread House

streets
in Bethlehem
Tagging into the connection
Baby fingers clasped tightly to its coattails
Adding longevity to him, perhaps

We have no right to speculate that
And yet, obscurely, on record, there the fact is,
doubling that
Connection,
To the consciousness?

To the consciousness
and we have not even started on apples
Falling or otherwise

Engage the
eye
shift the
dynamics
AEY-
RIE
I
R*is**
Ha-ha
Laughter ringing OUT

---

* *ris*—laugh (FR), pronounced "ree," long "e"

The beggar, across the glass in Paris—*pleading for a cigarette,* a simple thing really—he mimed a wavy line with his up-and-down mouth.

Did that to my face, he did
Picked me out as an easy target, for sure
Right outside my seat at the café
In Paris
Looked me in the eye
A *cigarette, please, Miss,* he pled
Making the wavy head movements and
puffing with his mouth
Just as if he were
No one said
the ghost of Richard Feynman
been much too long without a smoke, he had
pointing to some theory that picks up FROM THERE. Is it not so?
I am quite late to note this. Obvious, once connected to the CLUE.

Also, a wavy line was one of the five fundamental shapes to guess
in the Zener ESP cards of J. B. Rhine
And more importantly, *which of the associations was speaking to me*????

But then, I am thinking in terms of points. This was A
WAVE

Ava?
Perhaps
No
Doubt
Another
Mar
rune

In the style of the *Arabian Nights*, then, we insert this passage. It is a major theme, the major theme, of this book. But its winding tributary of a trail means that it tells its story in a lengthy way. For how many centuries has its stored up its documentation? All the centuries we persisted, totally unaware of its vibration, its location, its principles. This essay has introjected the clue—that if form has its DNA, what about nonform? Electricity? Does it too recognize some organizing principle? Does sound? What about—?

What might the organization detect as information? Instructions. Not wanting to "reconstruct" at every second.

As that day in the early 1990s, in exiting his room (studying the flea)—a pioneer after all, though invisibly, amidst the cigarette smoke—Klonsky emerged (precisely) INTO MY VIEW. A "roach" in hand, no doubt (oh yes, he shouldn't have but he did). Carrying this insight, half-vocal—in that way projected strongly—to impress how important (even, let me say, "all important") this moment was. As if there were ways to "stop" time in a person's mind or to press a button that insured they would remember.

Carrying in its own transmission vehicle the necessity of DARING TO PLANT its implication. Greedily snatching at the thought, really. Here, we are positing that in the seventeenth century the communicability of the germ was the *physical* dimension—the acted-out version (reported) of the transmissibility of the very pattern the discovery entered THRU.

And—bear with me—wasn't it that that the clownlike beseeching beggar, in his exaggerated miming, was trying to hint at himself, in Paris, in 1965? tunneling into time that day in Paris—asking for a light for his "roach," yes. Hailing THAT PART of me, which, too, wasn't here yet. Not exactly. So he used the symbol the message was in. Blowing an imaginary ring of smoke, miming that this was a guessing game, serious albeit.

His head tracing up-and-down waves.

Well, compare that to Feynman standing, himself with cigarette in mouth, not bobbing, but drawing—a wave. Speculatively, going way out on a limb, suppose (I might even speculate) that a "photon being" was trying to contact me and I recognized the sign. The energy signature of photon beings, or one in particular. And suppose—*we can suppose anything*—a photon had a consciousness if it was (or provided it was, and were they all?) a photon *being*, did they all share the same consciousness and even location? How would I know anything at all about it?

The wavy line, in our conjecture, said I did. It signaled me—as sure as electromagnetism carries signals, its message to begin, to speak. ON THIS MATTER.

But that's saying that not only do particles communicate through signals. They communicate through pictures. *And maybe get into our bodies to draw them kinetically.* But we've been saying that all along.

The designated emissary in Paris, just as if he were writing a blackboard diagram with a piece of chalk: the one where "an electron (e^-) and a positron (e^+) annihilate, producing a photon . . . that becomes a quark-antiquark pair . . . , after which the antiquark radiates a gluon"—made a wavy line. His bobbing head drew me to it.

Just as "nineteenth-century German chemist August Kekulé dreamed of a snake eating its own tail"—*after which he pictured the ring structure of benzene.*

Kekulé had two daydreams that led to his discovery, wrote Alan J. Rocke, in *Image and Reality*, as reviewed by Andrew Robinson in *Nature*—"the first in the summer of 1855 on top of a London omnibus, the second in 1862 in his apartment in Ghent, Belgium, while . . . writing a pioneering chemistry textbook."[21]

The "visual" side had "done it again."

"At every turning point, [Rocke] suggests," wrote Robinson, "early chemists used their imagination to visualize the constitution of the micro-world, leading the way in visual thinking."

And could anyone step through time through that very ring that had gotten used to presenting itself in a vision? For instance, step through a snake eating its tail to benzene to, even, the smoke ring of my beggar???

So we have found, a major plotline and statement, that we are to discuss the workings of a QUANTUM, OR UNIT OF STRUCTURE, CALLED ALPHA/OMEGA.

That in addition, this quantum (diversifying, becoming quanta of action) has a corollary, a second proposition, that is already researched in what we are calling the Flea Essay. These, to hold the book together for a time; to be the loom threads of Penelope, to weave space-time into Earth-time. To be the very binding, down the sides of the pages. We go on, returning to where we interrupted, after the preceding page. Rather, let us pause, to take up an entire new volume.

(Smile.)

&1L

Are we really discovering that "germs" of ACTION, of pre*conceived* and structured sequences—etc., etc.—can be sprayed or shot through the air (or we will get to how else) in the UNITS we put them into? Or somebody did. Thinking these were innocuous. When they were our "homing pigeons," carriers of our concerns—our future—in that before we knew it, if vulnerable enough, the world would pick up these "suggestions." Only, they weren't just suggestions, by any means. They were loaded and set up for triggering. They were bombs of a sort. Mental ones. Emotional. AND we had No IDEA!

✳

And I END in the consciousness in Zurich.

It cannot be true.

It is ALL THAT CAN BE TRUE. The consciousness I went into—

that was writing a book. How he showed me. How I arrived in the stadium. How he was projecting it into the future, when the future would intersect HIS CONSCIOUSNESS. It cannot be true.

It MUST be true.

POEM CODA

The universe came to visit me the other night

I have tried to record where it led me
Came twice
once on my eyelids
once over my head in a conscious dot

The Omega came to visit me
followed fast on its heels
the
Alpha
Finally recognized in all their disguise
their two roles
the Alpha as the Little Dot
the Omega the universe on my lids
Compressed,
Circling back
there it was again,
over-
HEAD
the Alpha
I had to figure it out
why they were there
who they were
Took me decades
And then, just now, I got it
Yes, yes
The compressed dot, the vast sky, what else?
beckoning me on the path to them
So many initiations
Pulled upward to a break in the ceiling above
Always the same
Always this
The dot to Begin

The Whole
At the End

Pursued by a baby universe? Really, you've got to be kidding me.
No, come back here. What do you mean, pursued by a baby universe?

Don't you know what patterns are?
Don't you know the energy in the tiniest atom?
Don't you know how powerful YOU are?
Well, if a tiny ball could compress the entire universe inside it
Trusting we would make good on its donation
I don't say sacrifice
Self-sacrifice
As it spawned the future of itself
Then what about us

Made in its likeness?
No?

I'm saying yes.
We are given this secret pattern
To compress and become
A world in a grain of sand
Explode and take the shoreline of the rivers with us
Chaos inside
Explode with our eyes shut
And start over
In the Archetype of
"To Begin"

The Alpha?

Standing right here
At your service
And beside it?
The Omega
Like a game of "kick the can"

The Omega moves away
—giving the Alpha all the room *not yet*
in the to-be world
but on the way
to express itself
in

So is that what happened to you?
that day you looked up and chose to follow the Little Dot?
I'll say

Hark, something passing by
coming in

what was in the Little Dot
Filled with past universes
—or only those to come?

Not only was the Earth once a baby

But so was
the baby universe
All snuggled up
Filled with hopes and dreams?
Yes
Memories?
That it had to discard?
Yes
No, not discard. Rather take with it as—?
Cards to play
If the going got rough
Tough?
Touch and go
—it held
Cards
U*p*—?
Up
Its—
Sleeves

The Little Dot had a sleeve?
Yes, and folks to
Pull on it
Behind the scenes—
If need be

So we're safe?
I wouldn't go that far, suspense did
Reign?
Yes, and
rain

The baby universe
expanded and expanded, reorganizing

Material
and as the dust
Oops particles
Settled
Looking at
the Earth
to-come
Swelled with satisfaction as the swirling stardust
Led inevitably to
Us
So that if we ever wondered if there were ETs among us
Well, we could just look to the remnants,
the expansions,
The unremembered memories of
The baby universe that
Mothered
us

They catch me off guard, these poems that
Want to be included
To tip
Their hand in showing their presence
Dusted-off
stardust
The same composition as
In the interior of
Us

So we are enquiring whether there was a parallel between the large numbers (the quantitative humanity) and the One, which—apparently—introduced its Start, its Big Bang, of a new idea in a CONCERTED CONCEPT.

Why, yes
Squeezed into a point, it rushed out
No yawns
Tight focus
our baby universe knew all about that
Ready micro-seconds later
to hit its stride
But what happened, the spread-out Alliit was in the
Compression

the spread-out old All,
could not lag behind
rush to get inside
The squeezed ball
Or
It
Died

We inherited it
If made in the baby universe's likeness
It was called
Karma
But
We can outwit it by
Understanding
Its
Purpose

That seems to be the pattern
One more I've
Figured out

No, been allowed to
See behind
In-
2
In two?
Yes, it was in twos
The All carrying the multitudes inside
The options
The masses
And the
Masses who
Lagged behind
As the ax fell
Oh, no
A strong incentive to
Join it
We pull the curtains on
And re-
Veal
Un-
Veil
How we are
Bound together
One way or
Another
Bound into the tight compression when it heads out
Into a new era or
In the tiny ways we
Pick up this
Initiative, this roadmap for
Joining
To-
gather

"Live your life as an exclamation rather than an explanation"!
Newton shouts—

breaking the sound barrier
The time barrier

What?
Not explain myself?
That's not how we do things here
many inhabitants of the Earth protested

but he was already gone
Fleeting past

I never explained myself.
The baby universe said
And look how far I went

Newton, we are told, said to live your life as an exclamation
One of the most daring things he ever prescribed for us
To do it
Live life as--?
Your life as
An
Exclamation

Exclaim it
That was the thing to do with it
Bellow
Roar
Cry out
Exclaim it as fact
Challenge others to join in
believe it
Your life

This motto you live by

An exclaiming
No explaining
not unnecessarily

Well look, Leonardo said,
How we say it in Italian
I say it
A *dimostrazione*
You put yourself to the test
You demonstri

How?
Through life's experiences

Fancy, aren't you?

Else, it doesn't count

Do you think anybody's going to understand you
—YOU—
unless you demonstrate it

you mean incarnate and illustrate myself?

exactly so
here's a drawing board
now sketch it
and then
for good measure
the essential part
you go out and live
an
exclamation
Go out and shout it from the rooftops

This is me!

Did you do that?
The baby universe showed me how
She put herself into the hands of the inhabitants
burying everything we could need, the secrets for us to find

Well, let's go looking for more secrets
Seems we could use some
On the next lap

Don't think we're stopping or slowing down yet
yet
So much more to create

※

JEF CRAB, drumming:

Nature only exists because of an awakened consciousness

MAH: How can that be? You must be saying the English wrong.
What do you mean?
Surely not that nature wouldn't exist except for an awakened
consciousness, that an awakened consciousness created nature.
Surely not. That's absurd.

JEF: What came before the Big Bang?

MAH: Oh, I see. You are saying that an awakened consciousness
preceded the Big Bang. Is that it?

Jef; But, Margaret, you are into the next book: *Stop All the Clocks;*
More Conversations with Shaman, Taiji Master, Rainforest Activist Jef Crab.
Our chats happen there. Lots of them.

Acknowledgments

My heart is made full by the inspiration, the spirit energy, that comes to visit and push me to write each day. Also, by those of you who read my books, including especially if you like to "come back for more." I am flabbergasted that that is the case, being of the Jungian point of view: he never expected understanding readers. And for him they came in flocks. Any readers I have, I am sure, their own inquisitive nature led them to me. And, fellow inquirers, I couldn't thank you more.

Also, of course, I thank all my closest family and my many kind and often fascinating friends. And the long-lasting friendships, soul communication and recognition that developed with teachers who once set me aloft into these inquiries by their fascinating clues as to where to go next, A few names jump out: Roland Verschaeve, Chris Van de Velde, Jef Crab, Jyoti and Russell Park. My light body founder channels, Duane Packer and Sanaya Roman. And where do I stop? Certainly not before a very special thanks to my parents, Rosa Lee and J. Henry Harrell, who always did their very best for me and filled our home with flowers, a Life model, and joy.

Notes

[1] F. David Peat, "Active Information," Ideas on Active Information - F. David Peat (fdavidpeat.com).

[2] David Seamon, Preface in *Goethe's Way of Science*, 3–4.

[3] Arthur Zajonc, "Light and Cognition" in *Goethe's Way of Science*, 312

[4] Seamon, David, Preface in *Goethe's Way of Science*, 2.

[5] Maria Popova, William Blake's Most Beautiful Letter: A Timeless Defense of the Imagination and the Creative Spirit – The Marginalian.

[6] Goethe, The New Britannica Encyclopaedia: Macropaedia, vol. 20: 138.

[7] Some slight difference in quoted language comes from an earlier edition of Britannica.

[8] James Gleick, *Chaos: Making a New Science*, 1987. New York: Viking, 163–164.

[9] Thomas Levenson, "The Truth about Isaac Newton's Productive Plague," https://www.newyorker.com/culture/cultural-comment/the-truth-about-isaac-newtons-productive-plague.

[10] Rahul Rao, Physicists spy X particle in Large Hadron Collider data | Popular Science (popsci.com).

[11] **Ibid.**

[12] Jennifer Chu, MIT News, Scientists make first detection of exotic "X" particles in quark-gluon plasma | MIT News | Massachusetts Institute of Technology.

[13] Daniel Garisto, The Universe Is Not Locally Real, and the Physics Nobel Prize Winners Proved It | Scientific American.

[14] Dani Rhys, Ancient Egyptian Scarabs - Significance and Origin (symbolsage.com).

[15] Paul Davies, *The Fifth Miracle*, 62.

[16] Britannica, "Career of Isaac Newton: The Optics," Isaac Newton - Scientist, Physics, Mathematics | Britannica.

[17] Dave Robinson and Chris Garratt, *Introducing Descartes*, 23.

[18] APS News, May 2000, vol. 9, nr. 5, "May 10, 1752: First Experiment to Draw Electricity from Lightning," This Month in Physics History (aps.org).

[19] Bread Street, London.

[20] "A London Inheritance," Bread Street - A Devastated City Street - A London Inheritance.

[21] Andrew Robinson, "Chemistry's Visual Origins," *Nature* 465, 36 (2010), doi: https://doi.org/10.1038/465036a. A review of Alan J. Rocke, *Image and Reality: Kekulé, Kopp, and the Scientific Imagination* University of Chicago Press, 2020.

Works Cited

BOOKS

Bohm, David. *Wholeness and the Implicate Order*. London & New York: Ark Paperbacks, 1988.

Davies, Paul. *The Fifth Miracle: The Search for the Origin and Meaning of Life*. New York: Simon & Schuster, 1999.

Elsasser, Walter M. *Reflections on a Theory of Organisms: Holism in Biology*. Baltimore & London: The Johns Hopkins University Press. 1987.

The New Britannica Encyclopaedia: Macropaedia, 15th edition, vol. 5. "Goethe." University of Chicago, 1992.

The New Britannica Encyclopaedia: Macropaedia, 15th edition, vol. 22. "Leonardo." University of Chicago, 1992.

The New Britannica Encyclopaedia: Macropaedia, 15th edition, vol. 24, "Newton." University of Chicago, 1992.

Ferris, Timothy. *The Whole Shebang*. New York: Simon & Schuster, 1998.

———. *The World Treasury of Physics, Astronomy, and Mathematics*. New York: Boston: Little, Brown, & Co., 1991.

Gingerich, Owen. "Let There Be Light." In Ferris, edited:378–394

Gleick, James. *Chaos: Making a New Science*. New York: Viking, 1987.

———Genius: *The Life and Science of Richard Feynman*. New York: Pantheon, 1992.

Gould, Stephen Jay. *Life's Grandeur*. London: Jonathon Cape, 1996.

Goswami, Amit. *The Visionary Window: A Quantum Physicist's Guide to Enlightenment*. IL: Quest Books, 2000.

Kane, Gordon. *Supersymmetry: Squarks, Photinos, and the Unveiling of the Ultimate Laws of Nature.* Cambridge, MASS, Perseus Publishing, 2000.

Klonsky, Milton. "Art & Life: A Menippean Paean to the Flea; or, Did Dostoevsky Kill Trotsky? pages 115–188). In Ted Solotaroff, ed. New York: Bantam Books. Reissued without illustrations in T. Solotaroff, ed. A *Discourse on Hip: Selected Writings of Milton Klonsky.* Detroit, MICH: Wayne State Univ. Press, 1991.

Krishna, Gopi. *Kundalini: The Evolutionary Energy in Man* with psychological commentary by James Hillman. Revised edition. Boston & London: Shambhala, 1997.

Oxford Family Encyclopedia. London: George Philip Ltd., 1997.

Robinson, Dave, and Chris Garratt. *Introducing Descartes,* 1998, New York: Totem Books.

Rocke, Alan J. *Image and Reality: Kekulé, Kopp, and the Scientific Imagination* University of Chicago Press, 2010.

Seamon, David, Preface. In David Seamon and Arthur Zajonc, eds., *Goethe's Way of Science,* A *Phenomenology of Nature.* New York: State University of New York Press, 1998.

Sfetcu, Nicolae. *About God in Newton's Correspondence with Richard Bentley and Queries in Opticks.* DOI: 10.13140/RG.2.2.16732.44162.62.

Smolin, Lee. *Three Roads to Quantum Gravity.* New York: Basic Books, 2002.

——Preface, *Einstein's Unfinished Revolution: The Search for What Lies Beyond the Quantum.* Kindle, 2019.

Smoot, George, and Keay Davidson. *Wrinkles in Time: The Imprint of Creation.* New York: Little Brown Co, 1993.

White, Michael, and John Gribbon. *Einstein: A Life in Science.* New York: Penguin, 1994.

Also by Margaret A. Harrell

More in the *Keep This Quiet!* Series

Keep This Quiet!

"Margaret Harrell's *Keep This Quiet!* offers an illuminating look at Hunter S. Thompson in full throttle trying to make it as a Top Notch prose-stylist. Harrell fills in many important biographical gaps. A welcome addition to what is becoming the HST cottage industry. Read it."

—Douglas Brinkley, editor of *The Proud Highway* and *Fear and Loathing in America*

"Memoir will likely please Hunter S. Thompson fans and appeal to readers with an interest in the beginnings of the post-modern era or the personal sacrifices involved in bringing serious written work to fruition."

—*Kirkus Reviews*

"With a solid dose of humor and another perspective on these writers from a personal friend, *Keep This Quiet!* is a moving read and much recommended to any literary studies or memoir collection."

—*Midwest Book Review*

"*Keep This Quiet!* is at once noisy, sensual, and word-drunk, as well as quietly intimate and full of Harrell's wonder at her luck. While most readers will come to this book for the Thompson content, in truth all the portraits here—all four of them—are compelling and often touching."

—W. C. Bamberger, *Rain Taxi Review*

"In the ever-expanding list of biographies and memoirs about Hunter S. Thompson, this latest offering, *Keep This Quiet!* by Margaret A. Harrell, is quite simply a breath of fresh air."

—Rory Patrick Feehan, PhD, owner of https://totallygonzo.org

"This is no ordinary book about or including Thompson. It's a memoir detailing personal relationships with three authors, the main focus being on Hunter . . . [I] must stress that this book, as a memoir is quite deep and holds the door open for the reader. While Hunter is a huge selling point, the book has the legs to stand alone."

—Martin Flynn, owner of https://hstbooks.org

Keep _This_ Quiet Too!

"A passionately written memoir that doesn't sit around being fit and proper and strait-laced . . . As a key to the lives of these three writers it is idiosyncratic and in an age where blandness is the norm it is a pleasure to go on her journey and find out a little about what makes these men tick and what drove her to them."

—Eric Jacobs, _Beat Scene_ (print) magazine, UK

Keep This Quiet! III—first edition: _Initiations_

"_Keep This Quiet! III: Initiations_ is as informative as it is entertaining and will be especially interesting to students of Jungian psychology and metaphysics . . . Very highly recommended for both community and academic library collections. Also exceptionally commended are the first two volumes in this outstanding series."

—_Midwest Book Review_

Keep This Quiet! IV—rev. edition: _Ancient Secrets Revealed_

"Margaret Harrell is a skilled professional writer with excellent ability to communicate and weave esoteric ideas about science, psychology, philosophy, and spirituality. Richard Unger's channeled hand analysis description of her as a 'grand synthesizer' was apt and accurate."

—Ron Rattner, subject of _Walks with Rob_: A _Spiritual Memoir_ documentary

"A puzzle master, Margaret walks us step by step through the process of her journey to that mastery . . . that wholeness of vision . . . so that we, if devoted enough, can also do the same. Margaret has injected so much LOVE into this work that, if you are open enough, it might just wake you up to your greater . . . even greatest potential."

—Joy Ayscue, co-founder of The Conscious Healing Initiative

The Hell's Angels *Letters: Hunter S. Thompson, Margaret Harrell and the Making of an American Classic*

Print copies available only from the publisher, Norfolk Press.com, or the author, https://margaretharrell.com

"Typed manuscript pages, scribbled notes, photographs, interviews, and all sorts of period ephemera relating to *Hell's Angels* allow the reader a valuable, behind-the-scenes glimpse into the making of this classic of New Journalism."

—Michael Dirda, the *Washington Post*

"Of course, there are already two collections of Hunter Thompson's letters available, but somehow they are even more enjoyable when read in the original form. Whether typed or scrawled in giant letters with a red pen, Thompson's correspondence is invariably annotated and corrected in his unique way, adding a layer of personality that was missing from the collections, as well—of course—as Harrell's explanations that provide further insight."

—David Wills, *Beatdom*

"*A big book, literally and figuratively* . . . a must-have text for any Hunter S. Thompson fan. Lavishly documented and illustrated with the actual correspondence that led to the publication of his breakthrough literary effort . . . The author, Margaret Harrell, who was Thompson's editor on his inaugural book, and her collaborator, Thompson's friend and associate poet Ron Whitehead, have succeeded brilliantly to create a fabulous present for you, or anyone in your life who admires Thompson's numerous achievements . . . It's worth every penny. *The* Hell's Angels *Letters: Hunter S Thompson, Margaret Harrell and the Making of an American Classic* gets five stars out of five! Bravo!

—Kyle K. Mann, *Gonzo Today*

"For anyone interested in reading about the serious, dedicated, and professional elements that made Hunter S. Thompson one of the most important famous—not to mention most infamous—writers of the twentieth century, this book is a must-have-behemoth to have on the shelf . . .

"This is more than just another write-up about Hunter S. Thompson, it's a NEW Hunter S. Thompson work."
—Leland Locke, Night Owl Narrative

About the Author

A three-time MacDowell Colony fellow, Margaret A. Harrell is also a book editor, cloud photographer exhibited in Europe as well as the United States, and an advanced meditation teacher in the LuminEssence school of light body and luminous body consciousness exploration, mentor to those wanting to maximize their potential. Harrell copy-edited Hunter S. Thompson's first book, *Hell's Angels*, and in 2021 included scans of his letters to her in the coffee table collectible *The* Hell's Angels *Letters* (Norfolk Press) in conjunction with US Beat Lifetime Poet Laureate Ron Whitehead. Other books she authored in the twenty-first century include the memoir series *Keep This Quiet!* I–IV, *Space Encounters* III revised: *Inserting Consciousness into Collisions*, *Beyond 3-D*, *Particle Pinata Poems*, and the artbook *Cloud Conversations*. In a varied, eclectic lifetime, which shows in her writing, she has lived many years outside the United States—in Morocco, Switzerland (at the C. G. Jung Zurich Institute), and in Belgium. A sought-after speaker, Margaret is currently behind the scenes in the thick of the organization of the 2025 New Orleans Gonzo Fest.

Thank You for Reading My Book

If you enjoyed reading it, I would deeply appreciate an honest review on Amazon and/or another platform. I will read every word you write and benefit from the comments.

Connect with me on Facebook, Linked In, and through my website, https://margaretharrell.com. Start a discussion with me.

You cannot know how much I appreciate your reading my books.